A Practitioner's Guide to Arbitration

Matthew H. Adler and Danni L. Shanel

AMERICAN BAR ASSOCIATION
Litigation Section

Cover design by Carolina Martinez/ABA Design

Printed in the United States of America.

27 26 25 24 23   5 4 3 2 1

ISBN 978-1-63905-312-4

A catalog record for this book is available from the Library of Congress.

To our parents

CONTENTS

ABOUT THE AUTHORS

Matt Adler is a senior partner at Troutman Pepper Hamilton Sanders LLP, where he is co-chair of the firm's international and domestic group. He is an adjunct professor of law, teaching arbitration, at George Washington University School of Law and has previously taught at the University of Virginia and Rutgers Law Schools. He publishes and speaks widely in the United States and abroad on arbitration topics.

Matt's diverse skill set and more than 30 years of experience make him a go-to attorney for commercial disputes in the United States and around the world. His clients turn to him for creative solutions in mediation, counseling, U.S. courtrooms, and arbitration panels. He handles commercial disputes before international, administrative, and judicial bodies, including federal and state courts, government agencies, and arbitration panels in the United States and internationally. Matt has led trial and arbitration teams on virtually every form of business dispute, including sales of businesses, supply contracts, intellectual property, insurance, real estate, lender liability, restrictive covenants, and sovereign immunity.

Matt began his career at a leading Washington, D.C., law firm in which he represented U.S. commercial interests expropriated by foreign governments. That brought Matt to government service with the U.S. Department of State, where he represented the United States in commercial and military claims against Iran at the Iran-U.S. Claims Tribunal located in The Hague, Netherlands. He later served as counsel to the Bureau of InterAmerican Affairs, where he worked on Central and South American foreign policy issues.

Matt has written extensively on the development of commercial arbitration law in the United States, especially in the wake of the explosion of U.S. Supreme Court cases on this subject in the past 15 years. He is the author of the law school textbook *Commercial Arbitration: Cases, Problems and Practice* (2d ed., Carolina Academic Press 2021).

Danni L. Shanel is an associate in the Troutman Pepper Hamilton Sanders LLP Boston office where she is active in international and domestic arbitration cases.

While attending law school, Danni served as a research assistant and helped research and draft memoranda on U.S. implementation of international government procurement agreements and aided in the completion of the second edition of *Commercial Arbitration.*

CHAPTER 1

An Introduction to Arbitration

If you find yourself at the beginning of this guide, chances are arbitration has entered your world view in some way. Perhaps you are responding to clients pondering whether they should include an arbitration clause in a contract draft, or you are examining the dispute resolution clause in an agreement under which you or your clients already operate. Maybe, less abstractly, you are staring down the barrel of an arbitration demand. Or, better yet, you picked up this book simply to learn about a fast-paced, quickly growing, ever-evolving legal practice area—in which case you're better situated than the rest of us. Welcome all.

What Is Arbitration?

Practically speaking, arbitration exists as an alternative to litigation. Although its practice has become more formalized over the past several decades, it still allows the parties much greater freedom of design. Arbitration allows participants to choose who they want to preside over their proceedings, what rules they want to govern, where they want to arbitrate, and who is allowed to know about it. In short, arbitration lets parties build their own courthouse.

Arbitration is a creature of contract. No party can be made to give up its right to litigation without first agreeing to do so. But just because arbitration is defined by its existence outside of the court system does not mean courts are not heavily involved. Quite the opposite, they play an integral role in compelling parties with valid agreements to arbitrate, enforcing awards rendered by arbitrators, and creating a body of case law detailing the most basic ground rules for the in-between. All things considered, the courts can't seem to leave arbitration be; in 2022 alone, the U.S. Supreme Court issued five new decisions regarding parameters for the practice.[1]

This judicial fascination with arbitration is not without good reason; nowhere in its 19 sections does the Federal Arbitration Act (9 U.S.C. §§ 1–19) actually define the word "arbitration." While this generally leaves parties with a great deal of wiggle room as to how they prefer to conduct their arbitrations, practitioners look to the courts for specific strictures. It is also worth noting what arbitration *is not*: mediation. Although often grouped together as alternative dispute resolution methods, arbitration and mediation are quite different. Unlike mediation, arbitration agreements are binding. In this sense, arbitration is much more akin to litigation than mediation. Once it gets started, the process becomes trial-like: parties present witnesses, move to strike evidence, and file preliminary briefs.

The following chart outlines the main similarities and differences between litigation and arbitration:

1. *See* Badgerow v. Walters et al., No. 20-1143 (decided Mar 31, 2022); Morgan v. Sundance, Inc., No. 21-328 (decided May 23, 2022); Southwest Airlines Co. v. Saxon, No. 21-309 (decided June 6, 2022); Viking River Cruises, Inc. v. Angie Moriana, No. 20-1573 (decided June 15, 2022); ZF Automotive US, Inc. v. Luxshare, Ltd., No. 21-401 (decided June 13, 2022).

Summary: Litigation v. Arbitration

	Litigation	Arbitration
Initiation	Summons and complaint	Notice of arbitration/ arbitration demand
Presiding individual	Judge assigned based on venue and court	Arbitrator(s), generally one or three, selected in the manner provided for by an arbitration clause or stipulated by institutional rules (with parties given input in many of these)
Binding outcome	Binding	Binding (a nonbinding arbitration clause is not arbitration)
Prerequisites	None; any party with standing may initiate a court proceeding	Mutual consent to a contract containing an arbitration clause
Discovery	Provided for under the Federal Rules of Civil Procedure	Not automatically provided for
Costs	Generally more expensive than arbitration (when taking into account discovery, testimony, and motion practice costs)	Can be (but is not always) less expensive than litigation
Privacy	Public record	Confidential
Time	Generally slower than arbitration; allows time for motions practice, discovery, and so on	Generally faster than litigation
Enforcement	Litigation outcome enforced by courts	Arbitrator ruling must be brought to a court to be enforced
Appealability	Appeal to court above	No appeal (except for limited circumstances enumerated by Federal Arbitration Act § 10 [see Chapter 12])

Hybrid or Consultation Clauses

Parties do not necessarily need to choose between arbitration and mediation when drafting a dispute resolution clause. The addition of a hybrid clause, also known as a consultation clause, allows contracts to require mediation or consultation between parties, usually within a certain timeframe, before the initiation of arbitration. Contracts can also stipulate to a "cooling off period," for example, 30 days, between the declaration of a dispute and the initiation of an arbitration for parties to allow cooler heads to prevail.

The sequencing of any hybrid clause is crucial. Practitioners should be sure to stipulate to mediation or cooling off first, before arbitration. It is also worth highlighting that a hybrid clause creates a condition precedent that must be satisfied before either party can compel arbitration. Ignoring a contractual requirement to mediate or observe a cooling off period will mean facing a motion to dismiss when trying to compel arbitration. Most importantly, any hybrid clause should be carefully and clearly drafted to avoid—as one author likes to put it—litigation about litigation.[2] Arbitration is a creature of contract, but where that contract lapses or fails to fix a gap, the courts will rise to fill it.

The following is an example of an crafted hybrid clause creating a condition precedent for arbitration:

> *If the parties are unable to resolve their dispute through informal resolution provided for in Section X, the parties shall, within thirty (30) days of the first meeting to resolve this dispute, attempt to settle the dispute by formal mediation. If the parties cannot otherwise agree upon a mediator and the place of the mediation within such thirty (30) day period, the American Arbitration Association in the State of New York shall administer the mediation. Such mediation shall occur no later than ninety (90) days after the dispute arises. If, after thirty (30) days after the commencement of mediation parties do not come to an agreement or agree in writing to extend the*

2. Professor Adler is vehemently opposed to litigation about litigation.

mediation deadline, the parties will commence a ten (10) day cooling period. If at the end of these ten (10) days both parties do not agree, they must commence binding arbitration under the rules of the American Arbitration Association.

Drafting an Arbitration Clause: An Overview

You have weighed the options and decided to include arbitration in your dispute resolution clause. Now what? You know that arbitration allows you to build your own courthouse, but what bricks are essential for the foundation? Any successful arbitration clause must include the "big three": (1) the "A" word—arbitration, (2) the requirement that the proposed arbitration be mandatory and binding, and (3) a defined scope.

First, any arbitration clause must stipulate that the parties wish to resolve a dispute through arbitration. Litigation is the default dispute resolution mechanism for any and all disputes, contracted or noncontracted. To circumvent this presumption, parties must explicitly provide for arbitration in their contract. Second, in order for courts to enforce an arbitration agreement, it must be mandatory and binding. To draft a nonmandatory arbitration clause would mean parties could opt for litigation instead, and nonbinding arbitration is not arbitration at all. The terms "mandatory" and "binding" do not necessarily need to grace your contract; instead, a party can illustrate the mandatory nature of an arbitration clause by including the terms "shall" or "must," rather than choice words such as "can" or "may." Last, it is imperative that the arbitration clause detail its scope. Do you want your clause to claim sweeping jurisdiction over any and all disputes arising out of the contract between the parties? Or would you prefer to only arbitrate matters related to payment under the contract? Do you want any matters regarding personnel to be litigated in the courts, or should only breach of contract be decided by an arbitration panel? These are all questions to consider when detailing the scope of a dispute resolution clause

Once you have included these three elements to secure enforcement of your arbitration provision, the rest of the clause can be customized.

Much like upgrades when buying a car, these additions to an arbitration clause can be tailored to meet the parties' needs. The following provides a high-level overview of these extras.

Institutional Rules

One key decision parties can make while drafting an arbitration clause is whether to apply a prefabricated, institutional rule regime, or to opt for "ad hoc" noninstitutional arbitration. Institutions such as the American Arbitration Association (AAA) and the Center for Dispute Resolution or JAMS (previously the Judicial Arbitration Mediation Service) provide standardized procedural frameworks for conducting arbitrations, as well as their own rosters of vetted arbitrators from which to choose. An added benefit of these frameworks is that their rules cover almost every possible issue that could arise between two parties in arbitration. Whereas drafters of an ad hoc clause may miss an unanticipated issue, leaving their contract open to interpretation (which can land the parties in court), institutional rules provide contingencies for everything from failing to agree on arbitrators to rules governing the collection of electronically stored information.[3] When parties opt for institutional rules, it is important they specify not only which institutional rules will apply to their arbitration but also *which version*; these institutions update their rules from time to time, so in order to avoid ambiguity down the line, parties should specify whether they wish to apply the institutional rules at the time of drafting or at the time of dispute.

The downside to institutional arbitration, of course, is that this institutional knowledge and support comes at a price. Additional costs are bound to increase with the size, complexity, and length of the arbitration.

Number, Qualifications, and Appointment Process of Arbitrators

Parties can also provide for the number, qualifications, and appointment process of presiding arbitrators. In general, parties default to

3. *See, e.g.*, AAA Commercial Rules R-12, R-22, and R-23.

choosing either one or three arbitrators. Each formation has its own advantages and disadvantages. A single arbitrator, agreed upon by the parties or selected by an institution, will likely resolve an arbitration more efficiently and less expensively than the alternative (arbitrators are compensated for their time, so naturally one is cheaper than three). Otherwise, a three-arbitrator panel might be advisable in complex cases with a higher amount in controversy, especially where parties might foresee difficulty agreeing on one arbitrator. In some instances, each party can nominate its own arbitrator who together in turn nominate the third. Other structures call for all three to be chosen by the parties from an institutional list, or for the institution to choose the third member. Where a contract calls for a party to appoint an arbitrator, it may be helpful to include a time limit, at the expiration of which the governing institution will make the choice for it.

Besides the number of arbitrators, parties can stipulate to an arbitrator's background or expertise. Is the nature of your agreement such that any arbitrator would need to be an engineer to properly understand the dispute? What about an accountant? Patent expert? Healthcare lawyer? This question is another parties should ponder while drafting their clauses.

Discovery

Discovery is not guaranteed in arbitration. If the parties so desire, they (or their designated institutional rules) can provide for this exchange. This is one add-on that is often left out of contractual arbitration clauses, mainly because parties find it difficult to nail down what type of discovery they might want in a hypothetical dispute before one even arises. After a dispute arises, it becomes even more difficult to agree on discovery given the adversarial nature of the parties.

Choice of Law

Parties can (and most certainly should) designate the governing law for their dispute, either in the dispute resolution clause or elsewhere in their contract. For example, parties might agree to be governed by the substantive law of New York or California. Parties that fail to designate a choice of law provision risk creating an entirely new dispute regarding governing law, which will likely need to be determined by an arbitrator before any arbitration can begin.

Injunctions

All parties—but especially those with contracts surrounding intellectual property or distribution rights—may want to provide arbitrators (or a court) with the ability to grant an injunction and preserve the status quo during a pending arbitration. This is known as an injunction carveout, and it can be added to a dispute resolution clause to ensure immediate action where needed. It is worth noting, however, that regardless of an arbitrator's empowerment by contract to grant injunctions, many circuits allow courts to issue injunctions to preserve a status quo while an arbitral panel is being assembled.

Form of Award

Unlike in litigation, there is no requirement that arbitrators put forward their reasoning for their award (decision) at the end of an arbitration; instead, parties can decide how much detail they want to see from their arbitrators. Would you prefer a short or lengthy award document? A short award takes less time to compose, but it will provide little by way of answers to the complaining party. A longer opinion will provide more insight into the arbitrators' deliberation process but take more time to complete. Most parties opt for a "reasoned award," in which arbitrators recount the reasoning behind their legal conclusion. A reasoned award is particularly helpful where parties plan to continue their business relationship post-arbitration and aim use it as a guide moving forward. A reasoned award is also helpful when parties seek to have an award overturned. Although 9 U.S.C. § 10 provides few instances in which a party can vacate a completed arbitration award, a reasoned award can help bolster an appealing party's argument.

Forum or "Seat"

The forum or "seat" of an arbitration, not to be confused with the choice of law, is the location where an arbitration is conducted. Although this may not necessarily match the location of the governing law, the choice of seat impact cannot be understated. While this decision holds more power in an international arbitration context, the main takeaway for domestic practitioners revolves around enforcement; the courts encompassing the seat are also the only courts through which a party can vacate an arbitration award. The law of the seat, rather than the parties' choice of law, also governs procedural issues. This matters more in international arbitration than in domestic, where any action under the Federal Arbitration Act is governed by the Federal Rules of Civil Procedure.

With regard to logistics, the location of the seat can influence travel costs, the availability of witnesses (although less so now with the acceptance of video conferencing technology), and arbitration general schedules.

Parties can choose any combination of these elements to include in their own arbitration provisions. A successful provision might look something like the this:

> <u>*Choice of Law*</u>*. This agreement shall be governed by and construed in accordance with the laws of the state of New York, without regard to laws that might otherwise govern under applicable principles of conflicts of law.*
>
> <u>*Arbitration*</u>*. Any claim or controversy arising out of or relating to this Agreement, including breach, termination, or validity of the agreement will be settled by arbitration seated in New York, New York, in accordance with the Commercial Rules of the American Arbitration Association (AAA Rules) in effect at the time of this agreement as modified by the following:*
>
>> <u>*Arbitrators*</u>*. Where the amount in controversy (excluding attorney's fees) does not exceed Ten Million Dollars ($10,000,000), the panel will be composed of a single*

arbitrator selected by the AAA. Where the amount in controversy exceeds this amount, the panel will consist of three arbitrators, one chosen by each party who together agree upon a third chosen from a roster provided by the AAA. Each party must select its respective arbitrator within thirty (30) days of the Arbitration Demand, past which point the AAA will select the party arbitrator.

Form of Award. The arbitrator or arbitrators will issue a reasoned award. Any judgment upon any award rendered by the arbitrator may be entered in any court having jurisdiction thereof.

Injunctive Relief. Notwithstanding the forgoing, each party shall be permitted to institute proceedings in a federal or state court of competent jurisdiction to seek temporary or preliminary injunctive relief to preserve the status quo pending the resolution of any dispute through arbitration.

CHAPTER 2

The Arbitration Presumption

Now you have an arbitration clause—is it enforceable? Can you challenge it? Should you? Would you rather be in court? How is your budget, both time and money, for fighting the clause? Or, assuming your opponent is attacking the clause because he or she wants to get to the jury, how is your budget for fighting *that* and instead trying to stay in arbitration?

If you are talking budget, then you are talking odds. What are your chances of success in challenging arbitration? In defending it? How much of a procedural "pre-game" do you want to play before fighting on the merits?

The odds in Las Vegas favor the casino. The odds in the U.S. court system favor proponents of arbitration. There is a body of law that has become increasingly well-developed over the last 40 years that repeatedly enshrines arbitration as a protected process and rejects challenges to arbitration on any number of grounds. While the courts are careful to say that they do not uphold "arbitration" but, rather, the "arbitration agreement," in point of fact that arbitration agreement—the contract, the arbitration clause—far more often than not withstands challenge. We call that here "the arbitration presumption." The house does not always win—but it usually does.

Before upholding an arbitration clause, a court must satisfy itself that both parties agreed to arbitrate in certain circumstances and that they anticipated the scope of those circumstances—in short, parties must point to an explicit *consensus* and *mandate.* That inquiry remains, but the test is a lenient one. It is, nevertheless, worth a brief review here should you find yourself in an arbitration challenge.

Consensus and mandate are the bedrocks of any arbitration agreement; there is no one without the other. *Consensus* refers to the parties' explicit agreement (generally distilled into a written arbitration clause). In order to enforce an arbitration agreement, a court will ask the following: Did both parties come to a consensus? Is there some agreement to arbitration in their contract? Does the arbitration clause withstand contract scrutiny? One party cannot force another to give up its right to litigation, and a court will not enforce an arbitration agreement to which both parties did not agree (more on this later).

If the parties *did* agree to arbitrate, the next question becomes, what *mandate* did the parties impart upon the arbitration panel created by their consensus? *Mandate* refers to the authority the resulting arbitration will have. Think of mandate a bit like subject matter jurisdiction—there may indeed be a valid arbitration clause, but does that clause apply to this dispute? A grower and a seller of fruit may have made a perfectly binding and unambiguous arbitration agreement by which any dispute that they have over the delivery of apples is committed to binding arbitration. But what if in year two, the parties expand their relationship to the sale of oranges, and in year three a dispute develops over oranges only? Is there a mandate to decide that oranges dispute? How far will and should a court stretch the arbitration agreement? Can the arbitrators rule on any dispute arising out of the contract? Or can they decide only issues regarding contractual breach? Do you want to call an arbitration to decide financial disputes, and if so, which ones?

Because arbitration is a creature of contract, the arbitrators' authority is only as great as that conferred upon them by the parties. Consensus is of no use without a defined mandate. Picture, for example, a pilot and a plane—each can exist separately, but only together will either ever leave the ground.

The Federal Arbitration Act and the Presumption in Favor of Enforcing Arbitration Agreements

The answer to the above questions, and one you should be conscious of as you consider whether and how to challenge (or defend) an arbitration clause, is that courts will stretch far. They will stretch to find consensus, and they will then stress to find a mandate—or, if you prefer lay terms, they will stretch to find an arbitration agreement and then stretch to find that that agreement applies to the dispute at hand.

Although Congress passed the Federal Arbitration Act (FAA) in 1925, it was not until the 1970s that courts truly began enforcing arbitration agreements. Then came *Moses H. Cone Memorial Hospital v. Mercury Construction Corp.*[1] In this seminal 1983 SCOTUS case, Justice Brennan, writing for the majority, finally solidified arbitration's place in the modern legal colloquium and proclaimed a "liberal federal policy favoring arbitration agreements."

Moses Cone has been a self-fulfilling prophecy. There may not have been a "liberal federal policy favoring arbitration agreements" before 1983, but *Moses Cone* certainly crated that policy in its aftermath.[2] As a result, courts—especially federal courts—*will look for ways to enforce the arbitration clause*. While the FAA is still being interpreted in new ways today, almost 100 years after its enactment, all arbitration questions can be approached in the same way. We first ask, is the contract "arbitrable"? In other words, does the arbitration clause need to be enforced? Was there a clear contract to arbitrate?

The Savings Clause

The liberal federal policy enshrined by arbitration is subject to exception, but it is critical to any challenge you contemplate to consider that the exception itself is contract based. A contract may not be arbitrable

1. Moses H. Cone Mem'l Hosp. v. Mercury Constr. Corp., 460 U.S. 1 (1983).

2. While otherwise beyond the scope of this guide, the word "liberal" has proven to be ironic. Generally speaking, in the decades to come, the court divided between conservative and liberal wings in applying *Moses Cone* to reject challenges to arbitration, with the conservative wing, led by Justice Scalia, authoring numerous opinions rejecting challenges to arbitration.

if it was concluded under a circumstance that might invalidate another like contract. Section 2 of the FAA, also known as the savings clause, notes:

> an agreement in writing to submit to arbitration an existing controversy arising out of such a contract, transaction, or refusal, shall be valid, irrevocable, and enforceable, *save upon such grounds as exist at law or in equity for the revocation of any contract.*

(Emphasis added.) These last two words of this clause highlight an essential caveat to the enforceability of an arbitration clause: if the arbitration clause was concluded through circumstances that would invalidate any regular contract, the arbitration clause, too, must be invalidated.

This is one particular way practitioners can attempt to avoid an arbitration. Look to your specific arbitration clause. Was it concluded under duress? While incapacitated? Through fraud? If so, it, like every other contract concluded under these conditions, is invalid.

The savings clause has given way to much litigation in the last two decades. Opponents of arbitration, and in particular the class action bar, have argued that the very nature of arbitration, in particular its general removal of disputes from collective actions in court, makes arbitration bad public policy and thus subject to section 2 challenges on the basis of inequity. Some states have passed laws that restrict arbitration's power to bind consumers or employees to individual arbitration, and then lawyers have challenged arbitration clauses under section 2 claiming that the clause is by nature illegal.

Those challenges have generally gone nowhere. The Supreme Court, in a number of opinions, has held that an arbitration clause cannot be challenged simply because it is an arbitration clause. There has to be some *other* problem with it. The clause must be shown to have been the product of fraud, or made by a party without capacity, or some other, plain vanilla contract defense. Circular attempts to outlaw arbitration and then invoke the savings clause have hit a SCOTUS brick wall.

These include public policy challenges. A now-vintage example is *Marmet Health Care Center v. Brown*, in which SCOTUS held that West Virginia could not pass a law exempting negligence suits against nursing homes from arbitration.[3] However noble the cause, *Moses Cone*'s "liberal federal policy in favor of arbitration" eclipses all state public policy objections.

That has led to very recent debate regarding arbitration and the #MeToo movement. When states began to pass laws exempting sexual harassment lawsuits from arbitration clauses (on the basis that employers should face public scrutiny), courts held fast, finding these state laws preempted by the FAA.[4] Acknowledging the clear need for litigation in these circumstances, Congress passed the 2022 Ending Forced Arbitration of Sexual Assault and Sexual Harassment Act, amending the FAA to allow any person (or group of persons) subject to predispute arbitration agreements to nonetheless file any sexual harassment or assault claims in court.[5] So steadfast was this presumption in favor of arbitration that it could be circumvented only through amendment to the act itself. In this way, the federal government embedded a public policy carveout within the FAA itself, keeping intact the nation's morals as well as its declared presumption in favor of arbitration.

Clause Construction and Interpretation

Like in any other contract, ambiguities within an arbitration agreement may also render certain disputes nonarbitral. For example, in *Lamps Plus v. Valera*, SCOTUS held that an ambiguous agreement does not provide the necessary contractual basis required to compel class arbitration. While the Court did note that ambiguities about the *scope* of an arbitration agreement must be resolved in favor of arbitration, the

3. Marmet Health Care Ctr., Inc. v. Brown, 565 U.S. 530 (2012).

4. *See, e.g.*, Latif v. Morgan Stanley & Co. LLC, No. 18cv11528 (DLC), 2019 U.S. Dist. LEXIS 107020 (S.D.N.Y. June 26, 2019); Chamber of Commerce of the United States v. Becerra, 438 F. Supp. 3d 1078 (E.D. Cal. 2020).

5. *See* Ending Forced Arbitration of Sexual Assault and Sexual Harassment Act of 2021, H.R. 4445, 117th Cong. (2022).

question of who may arbitrate will be resolved in favor of litigation (see Chapter 3). It is imperative, therefore, that drafters clearly enshrine a clear consensus and mandate in their contracts.

Venue

A word on venue: The Supreme Court has held that there is no presumption of federal court subject matter jurisdiction even though arbitration is the subject of a federal act. In *Southland Corp. v. Keating*, SCOTUS differentiated arbitration from civil rights laws or antitrust; unless the issue involves the FAA itself, therefore providing subject matter jurisdiction, diversity jurisdiction is required to reach federal court. However, federal law preempts state law on arbitration where the act does apply.

CHAPTER 3

Arbitrability, Severability, and Delegation

Consider the following hypothetical: Having carefully combed through the last two chapters in this guide, you now craft the perfect arbitration clause. It covers every contingency: it sets a seat, the number of arbitrators, which institutional rules should apply, the form of the award, the choice of law, forum, discovery requirements, a cooling off period, and even arbitrator qualifications for good measure, all wrapped up in a well-written contract. A dispute arises, and you are ready to invoke the clause. Except . . . the opposing party (incorrectly) argues that not just the arbitration clause but instead the entire contract is unconscionable and so unenforceable. What happens to your beautifully crafted arbitration clause? What about the rest of the contract? And more importantly, who decides what is and is not valid: a judge or an arbitrator? You have just run headfirst into the issues of arbitrability, severability, and delegation. Although at first these concepts sound theoretical, they can create very real problems for practitioners who underestimate their importance.

You have already been introduced to arbitrability, the first step in every issue analysis. A party must first ask whether a contract can be arbitrated. If the parties came to a *consensus* by agreeing to the arbitration clause in question, and provided the arbitrator or panel with a clear *mandate*, the clause itself is arbitrable. But what happens when you have a perfect arbitration clause contained within a contract that might be less so? Can a perfect arbitration clause survive an imperfect contract? Can a lawyer attacking an arbitration clause attack just that clause, or must he or she attack the entire contract?

This takes us to the oft-litigated, and critical-to-understand, subject of severability.

Severability

One unique aspect of an arbitration contract is that the arbitration clause is separable, or severable, from the contract in which it is contained. This means *the question of arbitrability is considered disconnected from the merits of the case that it will later govern.* If a party challenges a contract containing an arbitration clause in court, the court must first examine the validity of the arbitration clause, not the underlying contract. If the arbitration clause itself is not invalid (or even *challenged* by the opposing party), the court will compel arbitration. You may think that is silly because why should a party have to proceed in arbitration under a contract that itself may later be held invalid? You may think it is all the more silly because that (invalid) contract gave birth to the arbitration clause. It matters not.

The Supreme Court of the United States solidified this idea of severability in its 1967 case *Prima Paint v. Flood & Conklin Mfg. Co.*[1] There, the plaintiff alleged fraud in the creation of an overarching contract containing an arbitration clause. The Court faced a seminal question: if the contract was made through fraud, then could any part of it, namely the arbitration clause, be enforced? Perhaps counterintuitively, the Court said yes. SCOTUS held that if the challenge, in this case the accusation of fraud, was not aimed at the arbitration clause

1. Prima Paint Corp. v. Flood & Conklin Mfg. Co., 388 U.S. 395 (1967).

itself, but rather the contract at large, then the issue of fraudulent contracting was for the arbitration panel created by that contract to decide. In short,

> if the claim is fraud in the inducement of the arbitration clause itself—an issue which goes to the making of the agreement to arbitrate—the federal court may proceed to adjudicate it. But the statutory language does not permit the federal court to consider claims of fraud in the inducement of the contract generally.[2]

Thus, a basic arbitration rule emerged: challenges to a contract containing an arbitration agreement are decided by the arbitrator, but challenges to the arbitration agreement itself are decided by the court. This is illustrated in the flowchart below.

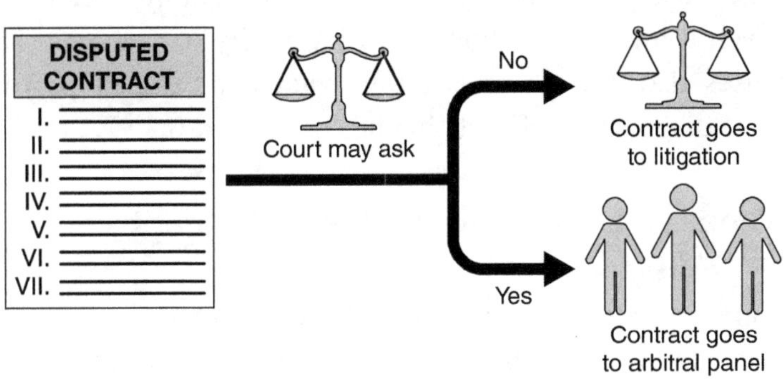

Delegation

The rule that courts, not arbitrators, had to decide challenges to arbitration did not prove popular with the arbitration bar. A solution emerged, founded in the notion that arbitration is at bottom a contract: parties could agree that issues of arbitrability could themselves be decided by the arbitrator. This is known as a delegation clause.

Through a delegation clause, parties can choose to assign the authority to determine arbitrability to the arbitration panel itself. This might again seem inherently counterintuitive; arbitrators exists only

2. *Id.* at 403–04.

through the clause that creates them. Those same arbitrators must now also decide whether their position was correctly created. If yes, the arbitrators lose their job, the arbitration is dissolved, and the parties can bring the dispute to litigation. If the arbitrators decide the contract is arbitrable, the case will continue to be heard in arbitration. And yet, courts accept and actively enforce delegation.

This adds a second principle to our rule above: **challenges to a contract containing an arbitration agreement are decided by the arbitrator, but challenges to the arbitration agreement itself are decided by the court UNLESS the parties expressly delegate the question of arbitrability to the arbitrator.**

Parties might choose to include a delegation clause for several reasons. It can prevent, as one author likes to put it, "litigation about litigation." A delegation clause eliminates an extra step and streamlines a dispute because parties must automatically bring any issue before the panel, even if a party questions the arbitrability of a dispute. Delegation clauses also lend themselves to privacy and can help prevent any part of the dispute from first being brought in court.

The "Clear and Unmistakable" Requirement for Delegation Clauses

Just as an arbitration clause is a separate contract within a contract (in this instance, one to forgo litigation in favor of arbitration), so too with delegation. And, as can be expected, delegation clauses come with their own set of specific requirements that must be present for them to be considered valid. If parties remember only one thing when drafting or opposing a delegation clause, it should be this: in order to successfully relinquish the right to bring the issue of arbitrability in court, courts require "clear and unmistakable" consent. Any ambiguity within a delegation clause will be construed in favor of the court.

SCOTUS made this strikingly clear in its 1995 *First Options of Chicago v. Kaplan* decision. There, the Court found the arbitration clause language did not "indicate a clear willingness to arbitrate [arbitrability]."[3] The Court noted that consensus among the parties was

3. First Options of Chi. v. Kaplan, 514 U.S. 938, 946 (1995).

required for this specific element because even though "any doubts concerning the scope of arbitrable issues should be resolved in favor of arbitration" (the main holding from *Moses H. Cone Memorial Hospital v. Mercury Construction Corp.*[4]), delegation clauses emerge in the context of an arbitration clause to which this presumption is already applied. The delegation clause, then, represents a separate contract within the arbitration provision. In interpreting this contract, SCOTUS held that "[c]ourts should not assume that the parties agreed to arbitrate arbitrability unless there is 'clea[r] and unmistakabl[e]' evidence that they did so." And yes, this rule application confuses more than just first-year legal students.

Given this new requirement, what exactly does a "clear and unmistakable" delegation clause look like? Consider these examples, all of which courts have found clearly showed both parties' consent to delegation of arbitrability:

- "If there is a dispute about whether this Arbitration Agreement can be enforced or applies to our Dispute, you . . . agree that the arbitrator will decide that issue."[5]
- "The arbitrator shall have the sole authority to rule on his/her own jurisdiction, including any challenges or objections with respect to the existence, applicability, scope, enforceability, construction, validity and interpretation of this Policy and any agreement to arbitrate a Covered Dispute."[6]
- "Other than issues related to the CLASS ACTION WAIVER, the arbitrator, and not any federal, state, or local court or agency, shall have exclusive authority to resolve any dispute arising out of or relating to the interpretation, applicability, enforceability or formation of this Agreement to Arbitrate, any part of it, or of the Terms including, but not limited to,

4. Moses H. Cone Mem'l Hosp. v. Mercury Constr. Corp., 460 U.S. 1 (1983).
5. Dunbar v. Airbnb, Inc., No. 19-00648 JMS-WRP, 2020 U.S. Dist. LEXIS 56828, at *7 (D. Haw. Apr. 1, 2020).
6. Kubala v. Supreme Prod. Servs., 830 F.3d 199, 204 (5th Cir. 2016).

> any claim that all or any part of this Agreement to Arbitrate or the Terms is void or voidable."[7]

All of these clauses include references to the arbitration agreement in which they are contained, as well as the fact that the arbitrator has sole power to determine arbitrability. As long as the clause contains these elements, the language utilized is up to the drafter.

Institutional Rules and Delegation Clauses

Your contract might have a delegation clause in it even if not in plain view. Most arbitration institutions now have delegation clauses incorporated into their rules, and so an arbitration agreement's adoption of institutional rules will silently incorporate (among other things) a delegation clause. The AAA, JAMS, and International Chamber of Commerce (ICC), for example, all fall within this category. Some are short and sweet, such as AAA Rule 7(a) ("[t]he arbitrator shall have the power to rule on his or her own jurisdiction, including any objections with respect to the existence, scope, or validity of the arbitration agreement or to the arbitrability of any claim or counterclaim"), while others are more careful to specify the instances in which a delegation will occur, such as ICC Rule 6(c):

> If any party against which a claim has been made does not submit an Answer, or if any party raises one or more pleas concerning the existence, validity or scope of the arbitration agreement or concerning whether all of the claims made in the arbitration may be determined together in a single arbitration, the arbitration shall proceed and any question of jurisdiction or of whether the claims may be determined together in that arbitration shall be decided directly by the arbitral tribunal, unless the Secretary General refers the matter to the Court for its decision pursuant to Article 6(4).

7. Chaudhri v. StockX, LLC (*In re* StockX Customer Data Sec. Breach Litig.), 19 F.4th 873, 877 (6th Cir. 2021).

In any case, parties who wish to adopt an institutional delegation clause should be explicit; while almost all federal circuit courts have found that general consent to institutional rules is sufficient to show clear and unmistakable consent to delegation, a few outliers are still are more hesitant.[8] The Seventh Circuit has not yet directly ruled on the issue, but it has held that contracts choosing an institutional rule regime incorporate those rules unless otherwise stated.[9] While it is unlikely a court will invalidate a delegation clause for this reason, practitioners should still take heed to confirm the stance in their respective districts.

Challenging Delegation Clauses

For those who find themselves challenging the validity of an arbitration agreement with a delegation clause, it is important to remember that because these are essentially specialized arbitration clauses within a larger arbitration agreement, they too are severable. The same rules therefore apply to challenging the delegation clause as do to challenging an arbitration clause. This means a party *must challenge the delegation clause itself to invalidate the delegation of arbitrability, rather than the arbitration clause as a whole*. Otherwise, the court will delegate the issue to the panel.

SCOTUS made this abundantly clear in *Rent-A-Center v. Jackson* (2010), where petitioners challenged the validity of a two-part arbitration clause. The first section provided "for arbitration of all 'past, present or future' disputes arising out of Jackson's employment with Rent-A-Center." The second, titled "Arbitration Procedures" provided

8. *See* Petrofac, Inc. v. DynMcDermott Petro. Operations Co., 687 F.3d 671, 675 (5th Cir. 2012), *citing* Allo v. High-Tech Inst., 559 F.3d 874, 878 (8th Cir. 2009); Qualcomm Inc. v. Nokia Corp., 466 F.3d 1366, 1372–73 (Fed. Cir. 2006); Terminix Int'l Co., LP v. Palmer Ranch Ltd. P'ship, 432 F.3d 1327, 1332–33 (11th Cir. 2005); Contec Corp. v. Remote Solution Co., 398 F.3d 205, 208 (2d Cir. 2005); Apollo Computer, Inc. v. Berg, 886 F.2d 469, 473 (1st Cir. 1989); *and* Riley Mfg. Co. v. Anchor Glass Container Corp., 157 F.3d 775, 780 (10th Cir. 1998). *See also* Airbnb, Inc. v. Doe, No. SC20-1167 (Fla. Mar. 31, 2022).

9. Commonwealth Edison Co. v. Gulf Oil Corp., 541 F.2d 1263, 1272 (7th Cir. 1976).

that "[t]he Arbitrator . . . shall have exclusive authority to resolve any dispute relating to the . . . enforceability . . . of this Agreement including, but not limited to any claim that all or any part of this Agreement is void or voidable."[10] The petitioner, who had clearly read *First Options*, challenged the arbitrability of the contract, arguing that the arbitration clause was unconscionable. But, because the challenged was the arbitration clause and not the delegation clause that specifically required issues like these to be arbitrated, the Court held that the issue of arbitrability was for the arbitrator to decide.

Arbitrability, Severability, and Delegation Flowchart

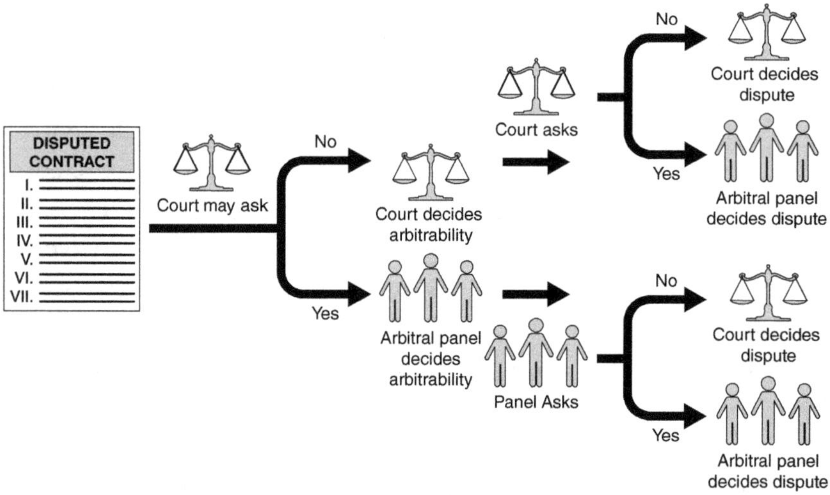

A Note on Class Actions

Class actions present a separate issue of arbitrability, one that has been frequently litigated at both SCOTUS and the lower-level courts.[11] Oftentimes, large-batch consumer and employment contracts (think credit card agreements, employment contracts with larger companies, and so on) will employ a short but effective waiver prohibiting the contracting parties from bringing any form of class or collective action.

10. Jackson v. Rent-A-Center W., Inc., 581 F.3d 912, 914 (9th Cir. 2009).

11. *See, e.g.*, AT&T Mobility LLC v. Concepcion, 563 U.S. 333, 336 (2011); Epic Sys. Corp. v. Lewis, 138 S. Ct. 1612, 1619 (2018).

These widespread class action waivers employ a one-two punch that, if upheld, immediately forecloses a large segment of the population from bringing claims arising under these contracts in courts.

These disputes involve a push on the part of plaintiffs to allow collective arbitrations and corresponding wishes on the part of defendants to arbitrate case by case, contract by contract, and plaintiff by plaintiff. Some states, consumer advocates, and others (famously including Justice Ginsberg) argue that these bars on collective action are just too efficient—so much so that they violate social policy and extend the reach of the FAA farther than it was ever meant to go. Plaintiffs, on the other hand, argue that any efforts to restrict agreed upon arbitration, including those clauses including such a waiver, are inconsistent with the FAA and must resultingly be struck down.

The overwhelming trend has been to disfavor class actions in arbitration, except where this right is expressly preserved in the arbitration clause (which these days is increasingly rare). The successful effort to keep class actions out of arbitration has resisted both attempted higher-level regulation and state legislation.

CHAPTER 4

Choosing an Arbitrator

One of the biggest attractions of arbitration is the parties' opportunity to choose their own arbitrator. It is also one of the most important decisions these parties will have to make. Unlike in litigation, where judges are automatically appointed—oftentimes without consideration for the type of parties appearing before them or the content of their dispute—arbitrating parties can pick their adjudicator. In so doing and thus in drafting that part of their arbitration clause that specifies the procedures for arbitrator selection, arbitrating parties can take into account the nature of their dispute, the expertise of their ideal arbitrator, and the number of arbitrators on their panel. This gives substantial input into the person who will decide the dispute and is far different than when one files a complaint in court and the judge is assigned randomly.

In Chapter 1, we briefly touched upon the elements that factor into arbitrator choice. This chapter will provide a more nuanced guide regarding the process of preserving arbitrator choice and the considerations that go into picking an arbitrator. Chapter 6 will cover how to challenge an arbitrator when an issue arises after appointment.

Arbitrator choice represents the ultimate contract customization option. Parties can tailor their agreements to provide for their ideal panel, complete with the skills necessary to best resolve their particular issue. Do you think you might want a panel of three people rather than a single judge on the bench to determine the outcome of your dispute? Draft it. Do you want to ensure those people have specific expertise, so that they can better understand the subject matter? Include such a requirement. Nationality, process of choice, and several other factors are on the table. For the competent drafter representing informed clients, arbitration offers the ability to eliminate much of the uncertainty surrounding the person who will eventually decide your dispute, long before the dispute arises.

Arbitrator choice arises as well where a specific arbitrator, or list of potential arbitrators, is proposed—perhaps by your client or your opponent or, as is often the case in so-called institutional (i.e., AAA and JAMS) arbitrations, by an institution circulating a list of qualified and available arbitrators. At that point, parties have the ability to perform due diligence and strike, rank, and/or select their choice. The same considerations outlined immediately below at the contract drafting stage on arbitrator selection should apply to that due diligence. Keep in mind, then, that you will have two opportunities to affect arbitrator choice: when you contractually state the arbitrator's required qualifications and when you make your actual arbitrator selection (or, at worst, ranking).

Arbitrator Background and Qualifications

Before putting pen to paper, parties should consider the profile of their ideal arbitrators. If all goes according to plan (with the dispute resolution process, of course—if you are invoking an arbitration clause, things have already gone less than according to plan, which is why we plan for the unplanned), who is hearing your argument? Are they understanding it? Do they bring their own implicit biases to the table that would hinder their full, unprejudiced consideration of the facts or your argument?

Think about the type of disputes that could arise under your specific contract and the scope of your arbitrator's mandate (see Chapter 2). If your case will likely stem from a straightforward breach of contract for the sale of widgets, most competent arbitrators will do. But if, for example, you gave your arbitrator the jurisdiction to hear intellectual property and trade secret disputes, perhaps you want to require that the chosen person has a background in that sort of law. Or maybe your company is dealing with highly specific products or technology, such as chemicals, medical equipment, or source code. Consider if the arguments surrounding these subjects might be better heard by someone with a background in your specific industry.

Practitioners are split regarding whether it is better to arrange for an arbitrator with a particular skill set. On one hand, parties are able to make higher-level, more detailed arguments to their adjudicators without expending the additional time or money required to explain or simplify certain complex ideas. However, arbitrators with their own expertise may (through no ill intent) enter an arbitration with their own preconceived notions about certain products or technology, often garnered through their own time in the field. At the extreme, this can crowd out the advocate's ability to shape their case. Another factor to consider is the universe of people with the proficiency you seek; stipulate to choosing an arbitrator with too precise a knowledge set, and the list of candidates will quickly shorten. This can also lead to issues of questionable impartiality when certain companies elect the same specialist arbitrator for all of their disputes.

When evaluating skill sets, do not forget that arbitration itself is a skill. Just because a lawyer is outstanding in their field does not necessarily mean that they will be an outstanding administrator of an arbitration. If you have a particular securities law case that you want arbitrated, by all means seek out a securities law expert—but it is advisable as well to research the number of arbitrations that securities law expert has served on. Have they been party appointed? A chair of the panel? Did the panel function on time? Did it get bogged down in scheduling difficulties? Were there a great many opinions or just one? Was the selected arbitrator a team player who could function with the other arbitrators? And perhaps most important, especially in the post-COVID era when alternate dispute resolution such as mediation and arbitration became more popular than ever and so good arbitrators booked up months in advance, does your selection have time on their schedule? Or will hearings be moved way back in the line? All of these are critical factors, now more than ever.

To avoid your disappointment and that of your client, it is critical to set down an honest schedule, one that appropriately anticipates discovery requirements, disputes over that discovery, and all other potential events, and then share that timeline with the arbitrator to ensure availability. An arbitrator who contemplates that he or she is free next summer for a three-day hearing may be less free the following fall for a seven-day hearing and even less so in resolving on short notice the five disputes that may arise between now and then. Be expansive, imaginative, and honest, and expect your arbitrator candidate to be the same.

Number of Arbitrators

Drafters should also consider the number of arbitrators needed to hear their dispute. In general, parties can provide for either one or three arbitrators, with each formation offering its own its advantages and drawbacks. A single arbitrator, for example, will likely resolve a dispute more efficiently and less expensively than the alternative; arbitrators are compensated for their time, so naturally one is cheaper than three. However, parties looking to use one arbitrator should take note: unlike in litigation, mistakes of law in arbitration are unappealable. No matter how off-the-rails the arbitration proceedings go, courts will vacate an award only in one of four enumerated situations provided for under FAA section 10(a) (see Chapter 12). Therefore, parties choosing a single arbitrator to hear their case assume the risk that their arbitrator makes this decision unchecked.

A three-arbitrator panel, on the other hand, may be advisable in more complex cases with a higher amount in controversy. A larger panel has more expertise at its disposal; it also precludes one arbitrator's opinion from reigning supreme. The creation of a three-person panel can also prevent problems where parties foresee difficulty agreeing on one arbitrator. Among the many other selection formats, parties can each choose an arbitrator of their own. Then, depending on the clause, the third and leading decision maker can be chosen by the parties together, by verdict of the two chosen arbitrators, or by an institution.

It is also important to note that parties can choose a hybrid option, as illustrated by the arbitration clause provided in Chapter 1. Skilled drafters may bifurcate their arbitration clauses based on the size of the amount in controversy, providing for one arbitrator by default and three only where the dispute exceeds a certain dollar amount.

Selection Process and Institutional Rules

Once you have landed on the ideal type and number of arbitrators, parties should agree on a selection process.

Option 1: Name the Arbitrator in the Arbitration Clause

> *In the event of a dispute, the parties select Mr. John Barrymore of the Maine Bar as arbitrator.*

This option is straightforward and simple; where parties can agree on a potential arbitrator, they can take advantage of the predictability and precision this provides. The downside here is that the nominated arbitrator might be unavailable when a dispute eventually comes to pass, because they are busy, conflicted, or no longer able to arbitrate for a host of reasons. Parties that opt for this option should include a default mechanism or backup clause if their chosen arbitrator is unavailable. For example:

> *In the event that Mr. Barrymore is unable or unwilling to serve, then the selection shall be made according to the Commercial Rules of the American Arbitration Association.*

Option 2: Specify the Expertise of an Arbitrator

> *In the event of a dispute, the parties will select a single arbitrator holding a doctorate in particle physics.*

As noted above, parties with complex subject matter at the heart of their contracts may want to take advantage of an arbitrator familiar with the field, its governing law, or the surrounding facts. As explained, this option is not without its disadvantages. Here too, parties should include a default mechanism if the parties cannot agree on (or even find) an available arbitrator with these qualifications.

Option 3: Where Three Arbitrators Are Desired, the Party-Appointed Arbitrators Choose the Third Arbitrator

> *In the event of a dispute, an arbitration panel will be composed of three arbitrators. Each party will select their own arbitrator [ALTERNATIVELY: two arbitrators will be chosen by the AAA]. The two arbitrators will then agree between themselves to appoint a third.*

When drafting a contract that calls for three arbitrators, parties have several decisions to make. They must either provide for agreement between themselves on a third arbitrator or allow the two party-appointed arbitrators to decide. The main advantage of this option is that both parties become involved at one of the most critical stages of the arbitration: choosing the decision maker. However, this option still relies on the ability of the choosing individuals to agree on a third arbitrator, which does not always happen. Alternatively, where neither the parties nor the party-appointed arbitrators can decide, a contract might delegate the decision to an institution. All institutions have rules addressing arbitrator selection in instances just like this.

If no institution has been named, FAA section 5 governs. It states,

> if for any other reason there shall be a lapse in the naming of an arbitrator or arbitrators [. . .] the court shall designate and appoint an arbitrator [. . .] as the case may require, who shall act under the said agreement with the same force and effect as if he or they had been specifically named therein; and unless otherwise provided in the agreement the arbitration shall be by a single arbitrator.

The senior judge of the district in which the arbitration is to take place makes all decisions enumerated under section 5.

Option 4: Parties Select Institutional Rules to Control the Appointment Process

> *In the event of a dispute, the arbitration panel will be composed of [one or three] arbitrators selected in accordance with the rules of the AAA.*

As more and more parties adopt institutional rules, this has become a very frequent means of arbitrator selection. It is, to a great degree, a hybrid that in some eyes presents the best of both worlds: expertise combined with party autonomy. The expertise is supplied by institutions who vet their "bench" and subject applicants for arbitrator status to a rigorous review and selection process. Persons "listed" as potential arbitrators for a panel by, for example, JAMS or the AAA, have undergone peer comments and a look at their experience, their ethical compliance, and their arbitration experience. Institutions will then provide the parties with these lists of qualified arbitrators, along with their biographical information. Party autonomy also comes in because once the parties receive the list, the parties "rank" the list (and in some cases can outright strike names) in order of preference.

It is possible to combine institutional choice with some of the other options outlined above. For example, parties can specify that they want a healthcare law expert but also opt for institutional lists with the expectation that the names on the list will all be within that expertise. Some parties may opt for an arbitrator off one of the five specially compiled AAA lists tailored to deal with commercial, construction, employment, labor, or international disputes. A party likely to face larger disputes can specify arbitrator selection from among the AAA large or complex matters list. Others might prefer arbitrators from the American Health Law Association or other content-focused organizations.

Moreover, adding to the parties' flexibility, pre-dispute choices like these are not set in stone. No lawyer can see the future, and each drafter can only wager their best guess as to the arbitral requirements of a yet-unrealized dispute. Therefore, just as parties agree on a pre-dispute arbitration clause, so too can they agree to change this clause to better serve the nature of the dispute when it emerges.

For example, if a contract prescribes an arbitration be conducted by three neutral arbitrators chosen off the AAA complex case list, but a dispute arises that would be better served by a single, mutually agreed upon arbitrator, parties can agree to proceed in this way. "Agree," however, is the operative term; if parties do not (or cannot) agree on a change to the clause, the contract prevails.

Even where an institution provides a list of clearly qualified individuals, parties must still whittle down the options to their ideal arbitrator, hence the emphasis on due diligence at the outset of this chapter. How do you choose? Arbitrator recommendations and background checks used to consist of firm-wide emails sounding something like "Have you ever had Mr. X as an arbitrator?" Thankfully, like many areas of law, this process has benefited from modernization. Now, parties can browse licensed online databases of arbitrators to aid in their decision. Like any other database, these systems often come at a cost, but for a party looking for the right arbitrator, they may be worth a look.

Client input is recommended at the outset. Clients should be aware of the institution's power to have this much impact in the selection process, as well as the difference in institutional rules. When drafting, make sure clients have the ability to view these rules first before picking one, as each institution's is slightly different. For example, AAA Rule 16 states that where an agreement does not specify a number of arbitrators and the parties do not otherwise agree, the dispute will be heard by one arbitrator only. AAA Rule 12 provides strict rules to follow in the choice of this arbitrator and outlines steps where parties cannot agree:

> (a) The AAA shall send simultaneously to each party to the dispute an identical list of 10 (unless the AAA decides that a different number is appropriate) names of persons chosen from the National Roster. The parties are encouraged to agree to

an arbitrator from the submitted list and to advise the AAA of their agreement.

(b) If the parties are unable to agree upon an arbitrator, each party to the dispute shall have 14 calendar days from the transmittal date in which to strike names objected to, number the remaining names in order of preference, and return the list to the AAA. [. . .] From among the persons who have been approved on both lists, and in accordance with the designated order of mutual preference, the AAA shall invite the acceptance of an arbitrator to serve. If the parties fail to agree [. . .] the AAA shall have the power to make the appointment from among other members of the National Roster without the submission of additional lists.

The JAMS rules contain a similar selection process to that of the AAA. The ICC rules, however, allow parties to bring their own out-of-institution arbitrators to the table and offer 15 days to do so:

* * *

(3) Where the parties have not agreed upon the number of arbitrators, the Court shall appoint a sole arbitrator, save where it appears to the Court that the dispute is such as to warrant the appointment of three arbitrators. In such case, the claimant shall nominate an arbitrator within 15 days from receipt of the notification of the decision of the Court, and the respondent shall nominate an arbitrator within 15 days from receipt of the notification of the nomination made by the claimant. If a party fails to nominate an arbitrator, the appointment shall be made by the Court.

(4) **Sole Arbitrator** Where the parties have agreed that the dispute shall be resolved by a sole arbitrator, they may, by agreement, nominate the sole arbitrator for confirmation. If the parties fail to nominate a sole arbitrator within 30 days from the date when the claimant's Request for Arbitration has been received by the other party or parties, or within such additional time as may be allowed by the Secretariat, the sole arbitrator shall be appointed by the Court.

(5) **Three Arbitrators** Where the parties have agreed that the dispute shall be resolved by three arbitrators, each party shall nominate in the Request and the Answer, respectively, one arbitrator for confirmation. If a party fails to nominate an arbitrator, the appointment shall be made by the Court.

(6) Where the dispute is to be referred to three arbitrators, the third arbitrator, who will act as president of the arbitral tribunal, shall be appointed by the Court, unless the parties have agreed upon another procedure for such appointment [. . . .] Should such procedure not result in a nomination within 30 days from the confirmation or appointment of the co-arbitrators or any other time limit agreed by the parties or fixed by the Court, the third arbitrator shall be appointed by the Court.

Time Limits

Whether stipulating to a one- or three-person panel, drafters should be prepared to set limits on the amount of time each side has to put forward its choice for arbitrator. Not only does this provide incentive and prevent one side from holding the arbitration procession hostage if they fail (or refuse) to make a timely choice, but also it rewards those that read their contracts closely. Oftentimes these clauses will give the late-choosing party's decision to an institution or other neutral party, potentially proving the timely party with a leg up.

Drafting Examples

A detailed arbitration clause taking into account everything discussed above might look something like the following. Keep in mind that this clause can be as detailed or as broad as the parties want. Also, if an unprovided-for situation arises, the clause can offer for institutional rules to fill in the gaps. One point that cannot be stressed enough is the importance of precision in drafting. To avoid potential arguments about language down the line, be clear and to the point.

> *<u>Arbitrators</u>. Where the amount in controversy (excluding attorney's fees) does not exceed Ten Million Dollars ($10,000,000), the panel will be composed of a single arbitrator selected by the AAA. Where the amount in controversy exceeds this amount, the panel will consist of three arbitrators, one chosen by each party who together agree upon a third chosen from a roster provided by the AAA. Each party must select their respective arbitrator within thirty (30) days of the Arbitration Demand, past which point the AAA will select the party arbitrator.*

A Note on the Importance of Diversity

As much as we would like to believe otherwise, background can play a large part in arbitrator impartiality. Arbitrators are as fallible as any other adjudicator. It is precisely for this reason that institutions such as the AAA allow parties from disparate countries to request a neutral, third-nationality arbitrator for the resolution of their disputes (AAA Rule 15). And while these institutions acknowledge the importance of arbitrator background and work to keep lists of skilled decision makers at their disposal, these lists are still notoriously nondiverse. So much so, in fact, that in 2018, Jay-Z famously sued the AAA for forcing him to choose from a list of majority-white arbitrators, which he argued discriminated against him on the basis of race in violation of New York's Equal Protection Clause.[1] He won, and was allowed to submit his own arbitrator list.

Historically speaking, the arbitrator pool has been carefully drawn from those with enough time to become experts in their field; think retired judges, well-known lawyers with established practices, and the like. Given historical barriers to entry into law—and the fact that only in 2016 did enrollment of women in law school slightly exceed that

1. *See* Carter et al. v. Inconix Brand Group Inc. et al., Index No. 655894/2018, Supreme Court of the State of New York County of New York.

of men for the first time—those comprising this list have long been majority male and majority white.[2]

While this is changing (the AAA reports that 29 percent of its panel currently comprises women and racially and ethnically diverse adjudicators[3]), it is doing so slowly. But changes are in the wind and many clients, driven by corporate values and their own investor imperatives, are themselves encouraging their counsel to choose arbitrators with diversity in mind. These authors would therefore be remiss not to encourage those now finding themselves within the arbitration field, in either writing or interpreting an arbitration clause, to pay close attention to the composition of the institutions you contract with, the lists you pick from, and the arbitrators you choose. Choosing to diversify these areas—bringing different lived experiences, expertise, and perspectives to the table—can only serve to improve the quality an impartiality of arbitrations for all involved.

---

2. *See Women Make Up Majority of U.S. Law Students for First Time*, N.Y. Times (Dec. 16, 2016), https://www.nytimes.com/2016/12/16/business/dealbook/women-majority-of-us-law-students-first-time.html.

3. *See Diversity and Inclusion*, Am. Arbitration. Assoc., https://www.adr.org/diversity-and-inclusion/panel.

CHAPTER 5

Challenging Arbitrator Selection

While it can be one of the most attractive elements of arbitration (and indeed, for some parties, the sole reason they opt for this type of dispute resolution), choosing your adjudicator doesn't always work out according to plan. Picture this: after both parties agreed on a single arbitrator to decide their dispute, the chosen person discloses information about their connections that bring their impartiality into question. Or even worse, you unearth new unsavory information about this person—halfway through (or even after) the arbitration—that means they almost certainly leans to one side. Now that you've made your arbitrator choice, do you have to stick with it? And if you can raise an alarm, when should you do so? Similar questions apply to arbitrators. Where does their expertise end and potential bias begin? What are their disclosure obligations? We explore these questions below.

FAA Section 10(a)(2) and "Evident Partiality"

We noted in Chapter 5 that selecting the right arbitrator is important for several reasons, but perhaps most important is the simple fact that you are stuck with your arbitrator. Bad arbitrators can do more lasting damage than bad judges. A judge can ultimately be overturned on appeal. An arbitrator can almost never be overturned on appeal. Once an arbitrator provides their award, it can only be vacated for a very narrow set of reasons as set out by FAA section 10(a). That provision provides:

> In any of the following cases the United States court in and for the district wherein the award was made may make an order vacating the award upon the application of any party to the arbitration—
>
> (1) where the award was procured by corruption, fraud, or undue means;
>
> (2) *where there was evident partiality or corruption in the arbitrators, or either of them;*
>
> (3) where the arbitrators were guilty of misconduct in refusing to postpone the hearing, upon sufficient cause shown, or in refusing to hear evidence pertinent and material to the controversy; or of any other misbehavior by which the rights of any party have been prejudiced; or
>
> (4) where the arbitrators exceeded their powers, or so imperfectly executed them that a mutual, final, and definite award upon the subject matter submitted was not made.[1]

(Emphasis added.) Section 2 is the focus of this chapter. Simply stated, arbitrator bias is a reason to overturn an award, but legal error in the award is not. Bias is one of the very few exceptions to enforcement, which is all the more reason to get the choice right at the start and remain vigilant about arbitrator independence throughout.

Having provided "evident partiality or corruption" as a grounds for disqualification, however, the FAA unfortunately fails to define this term; its meaning has been left entirely to the courts. SCOTUS first took its one and only swing at defining "evident partiality" in

1. It is important to note that no part of section 10(a) allows for vacation of an award based on the erroneous application of fact or law. This is yet another reason choosing the right arbitrator is so important. Unless an award was procured by fraud, with evident partiality, the refusal to hear evidence, or exceeding of arbitrator mandate as contracted by the parties, an arbitrator's decision stands. For a more in-depth discussion of vacating an arbitration award, see Chapter 12.

1968, with *Commonwealth Coatings v. Continental Cas.*[2] There, a subcontractor painter sued a prime contractor's sureties over nonpayment for a job. In accordance with the parties' contract, each side selected an arbitrator, who together chose a third neutral head. It was later determined that the third arbitrator had worked as a consultant for the prime contractor, who in turn had paid him $12,000 in fees over several years. The Court ultimately held that arbitrators have a duty to disclose any dealings that might provide even the appearance of bias; failure to do so rises to the level of evident partiality.

Arbitrators and arbitration counsel and other consumers nationwide have Justice White to thank for providing a bit more clarity here. In his *Commonwealth Coatings* concurrence, Justice White noted that while arbitrators—often with substantial past business relationships of their own—could not be expected to maintain the same level of impartiality expected of, say, a judge, "if the arbitrators err on the side of disclosure, *as they should*, it will not be difficult for courts to identify those undisclosed relationships which are too insubstantial to warrant vacating an award" (emphasis added).[3] Justice White therefore set the gold standard for arbitrator disclosure over the next 50 years: when in doubt, disclose it out. Failing to disclose, therefore, became a red flag for courts searching for evident partiality violations.

Commonwealth Coatings, now over 50 years old, remains the only substantial SCOTUS decision interpreting evident partiality. As result, the majority of our modern guidance regarding its definition comes from the lower courts. These courts have provided us with several cases explaining where exactly an arbitrator crosses the line. In 2014, for example, the Texas Supreme Court refused to enforce an arbitration award in *Tenaska Energy, LLC v. Ponderosa Pine Energy, LLC*, after an arbitrator failed to disclose that his litigation services company was actively pursuing business with counsel for one of the parties. Obviously expecting a windfall from a biased arbitrator, that same counsel changed its fee arrangement with the arbitrator's company from an hourly rate to a contingency fee. Most courts are still loath to

2. Commonwealth Coatings v. Continental Cas. Co., 393 U.S. 145 (1968).
3. *Id.* at 231.

automatically assume partiality, however. Take *Golden v. O'Melveny & Meyers*, for example, in which a California district court enforced the arbitrator's award, even after O'Melveny denied the arbitrator's son a position at the firm.

Institutional Rules on Disclosure

The case law does make clear that the touchstone of analysis in arbitrator bias cases is disclosure. Advising the parties up front of relationships, and getting their consent to the arbitrator's service notwithstanding those relationships, is an obvious solution to the potential conflict. At the other end of the spectrum, the failure to disclose can be seen as bias in and of itself, even if the nondisclosed fact would not in and of itself lead to a conflict. The rule for arbitrators is simple: disclose, disclose, disclose.

Fair enough, but disclose *what?* When is a relationship too unimportant, too remote in time, too immaterial, to merit omission from a disclosure form? What if the arbitrator had gone to summer camp with opposing counsel? Law school? What if their mothers were business partners? What if their law firm had a merger which took place after the arbitration? We are getting close, aren't we?

In an effort to clarify the inherent murkiness of arbitrator disclosure and ensure arbitration impartiality, arbitral institutions have attempted to distill the judicial discourse into clear-cut rules. Many of these institutions have integrated disclosure requirements into their regimes with varying degrees of specificity. The following examples illustrate just three different ways these organizations require disclosures.

AAA Rule 18: Disclosure

(a) Any person appointed or to be appointed as an arbitrator, as well as the parties and their representatives, shall disclose to the AAA any circumstance likely to give rise to justifiable doubt as to the arbitrator's impartiality or independence, including any bias or any financial or personal interest in the result of the arbitration or any past or present relationship with the parties or their representatives. Such obligation shall remain in effect throughout the arbitration. Failure on the part of a party or a representative to comply with the requirements of this Rule may result in the waiver of the right to object to an arbitrator in accordance with Rule R-42. Rules Amended and Effective September 1, 2022. COMMERCIAL RULES 21

(b) Upon receipt of such information from the arbitrator or another source, the AAA shall communicate the information to the parties and, if it deems it appropriate to do so, to the arbitrator and others.

(c) Disclosure of information pursuant to this Rule R-18 is not an indication that the arbitrator considers the disclosed circumstance likely to affect impartiality or independence.

AAA Rule 19: Disqualification of Arbitrator

(a) Any arbitrator shall be impartial and independent and shall perform his or her duties with diligence and in good faith, and shall be subject to disqualification for:
   i. partiality or lack of independence
   ii. inability or refusal to perform his or her duties with diligence and in good faith, and
   iii. any grounds for disqualification provided by applicable law.

(b) The parties may agree in writing, however, that arbitrators directly appointed by a party pursuant to Rule R-14 shall be non-neutral, in which case such arbitrators need not be impartial or independent and shall not be subject to disqualification for partiality or lack of independence.

(c) Upon objection of a party to the continued service of an arbitrator, or on its own initiative, the AAA shall determine whether the arbitrator should be disqualified on the grounds set out above, and shall inform the parties of its decision, which decision shall be conclusive.

ICC Rule 11: The Arbitral Tribunal—General Provisions

(1) Every arbitrator must be and remain impartial and independent of the parties involved in the arbitration.

(2) Before appointment or confirmation, a prospective arbitrator shall sign a statement of acceptance, availability, impartiality and independence. The prospective arbitrator shall disclose in writing to the Secretariat any facts or circumstances which might be of such a nature as to call into question the arbitrator's independence in the eyes of the parties, as well as any circumstances that could give rise to reasonable doubts as to the arbitrator's impartiality. The Secretariat shall provide such information to the parties in writing and fix a time limit for any comments from them.

(3) An arbitrator shall immediately disclose in writing to the Secretariat and to the parties any facts or circumstances of a similar nature to those referred to in Article 11(2) concerning the arbitrator's impartiality or independence which may arise during the arbitration.

(4) The decisions of the Court as to the appointment, confirmation, challenge or replacement of an arbitrator shall be final.

(5) By accepting to serve, arbitrators undertake to carry out their responsibilities in accordance with the Rules.

(6) Insofar as the parties have not provided otherwise, the arbitral tribunal shall be constituted in accordance with the provisions of Articles 12 and 13.

(7) In order to assist prospective arbitrators and arbitrators in complying with their duties under Articles 11(2) and 11(3), each party must promptly inform the Secretariat, the arbitral tribunal and the other parties, of the existence

and identity of any non-party which has entered into an arrangement for the funding of claims or defenses and under which it has an economic interest in the outcome of the arbitration.

JAMS Rule 15: Arbitrator Selection, Disclosures, and Replacement

* * *

(h) Any disclosures regarding the selected Arbitrator shall be made as required by law or within ten (10) calendar days from the date of appointment. Such disclosures may be provided in electronic format, provided that JAMS will produce a hard copy to any Party that requests it. The Parties and their representatives shall disclose to JAMS any circumstance likely to give rise to justifiable doubt as to the Arbitrator's impartiality or independence, including any bias or any financial or personal interest in the result of the Arbitration or any past or present relationship with the Parties or their representatives. The obligation of the Arbitrator, the Parties and their representatives to make all required disclosures continues throughout the Arbitration process.

(i) At any time during the Arbitration process, a Party may challenge the continued service of an Arbitrator for cause. The challenge must be based upon information that was not available to the Parties at the time the Arbitrator was selected. A challenge for cause must be in writing and exchanged with opposing Parties, who may respond within seven (7) calendar days of service of the challenge. JAMS shall make the final determination as to such challenge. Such determination shall take into account the materiality of the facts and any prejudice to the Parties. That decision will be final.

(j) Where the Parties have agreed that a Party-appointed Arbitrator is to be non-neutral, that Party-appointed Arbitrator

> is not obliged to withdraw if requested to do so only by the Party that did not appoint that Arbitrator.

In addition to codifying these requirements, many institutions require their arbitrators to comply with a separate Code of Ethics, providing additional guidance on how to do so. For example, in September of 2019, the AAA published a set of short disclosure guidelines that would apply to all arbitrators. In addition to the general instructions contained in their rule packet, the AAA tells arbitrators that they *must* disclose:

> Any circumstance likely to give rise to justifiable doubt as to your impartiality or independence (per AAA rules); Any interest or relationship that might create an appearance of partiality (per the Code of Ethics); Any applicable statutes pertaining to arbitrator disclosures.
>
> Financial—As to any party, attorney, witness and other arbitrator involved in this case, you must disclose any: Financial interest that is direct (existing or past) or indirect (existing or past).
>
> Relational—You must disclose any relationships you have with any party, attorney, witness and other arbitrator involved in this case—this includes relationships with their:; Families or household members; Current employers; Partners; Professional and/or business associates.[4]

The International Bar Association Red, Orange, and Green Lists

While courts have made it clear that an arbitrator must err on the side of disclosure, arbitrators cannot constantly be expected to, as the Court put it in *Commonwealth*, share an "unexpurgated business biography" each time they are called to adjudicate. The institutional rules above provide guidelines, but what specific instances truly require

---

4. *Disclosure Guidelines for Serving on American Arbitration Association Cases*, Am. Arbitration Assoc., *available at* https://www.adr.org/sites/default/files/document_repository/Disclosure_Guidelines.pdf.

disclosure? As it turns out, the International Bar Association took it upon themselves in 2014 to create the color-coded conflict of interest list provided for here in full below.[5] Circumstances in Green represent situations in which, objectively, no actual conflict of interest exists, and therefore arbitrators do not need to disclose. The Orange list, on the other hand, encompasses connections that, based on the specific facts of a case, may give rise to the doubts as to the arbitrator's impartiality. Connections making it to the Red list not only require disclosure but also most likely disqualify an arbitrator from the position unless waived by the prejudiced party.

1. Nonwaivable Red List

1.1 There is an identity between a party and the arbitrator, or the arbitrator is a legal representative or employee of an entity that is a party in the arbitration.
1.2 The arbitrator is a manager, director or member of the supervisory board, or has a controlling influence on one of the parties or an entity that has a direct economic interest in the award to be rendered in the arbitration.
1.3 The arbitrator has a significant financial or personal interest in one of the parties, or the outcome of the case.
1.4 The arbitrator or his or her firm regularly advises the party, or an affiliate of the party, and the arbitrator or his or her firm derives significant financial income therefrom.

2. Waivable Red List

2.1 Relationship of the arbitrator to the dispute 2.1.1 The arbitrator has given legal advice, or provided an expert opinion, on the dispute to a party or an affiliate of one of the parties. 2.1.2 The arbitrator had a prior involvement in the dispute.

5. For complete guidelines, *see* INT'L BAR ASSOC., IBA GUIDELINES ON CONFLICTS OF INTEREST IN INTERNATIONAL ARBITRATION, adopted by resolution of the IBA Council Oct. 23, 2014, *available at* https://www.ibanet.org/MediaHandler?id=e2fe5e72-eb14-4bba-b10d-d33dafee8918.

2.2 Arbitrator's direct or indirect interest in the dispute

2.2.1 The arbitrator holds shares, either directly or indirectly, in one of the parties, or an affiliate of one of the parties, this party or an affiliate being privately held.

2.2.2 A close family member of the arbitrator has a significant financial interest in the outcome of the dispute.

2.2.3 The arbitrator, or a close family member of the arbitrator, has a close relationship with a non-party who may be liable to recourse on the part of the unsuccessful party in the dispute.

2.3 Arbitrator's relationship with the parties or counsel

2.3.1 The arbitrator currently represents or advises one of the parties, or an affiliate of one of the parties.

2.3.2 The arbitrator currently represents or advises the lawyer or law firm acting as counsel for one of the parties.

2.3.3 The arbitrator is a lawyer in the same law firm as the counsel to one of the parties.

2.3.4 The arbitrator is a manager, director or member of the supervisory board, or has a controlling influence in an affiliate of one of the parties, if the affiliate is directly involved in the matters in dispute in the arbitration.

2.3.5 The arbitrator's law firm had a previous but terminated involvement in the case without the arbitrator being involved himself or herself.

2.3.6 The arbitrator's law firm currently has a significant commercial relationship with one of the parties, or an affiliate of one of the parties.

2.3.7 The arbitrator regularly advises one of the parties, or an affiliate of one of the parties, but neither the arbitrator nor his or her firm derives a significant financial income therefrom.

2.3.8 The arbitrator has a close family relationship with one of the parties, or with a manager, director or member of the supervisory board, or any person having a controlling influence in one of the parties, or an affiliate of one of the parties, or with a counsel representing a party.

2.3.9 A close family member of the arbitrator has a significant financial or personal interest in one of the parties, or an affiliate of one of the parties.

3. Orange List

3.1 Previous services for one of the parties or other involvement in the case 3.1.1 The arbitrator has, within the past three years, served as counsel for one of the parties, or an affiliate of one of the parties, or has previously advised or been consulted by the party, or an affiliate of the party, making the appointment in an unrelated matter, but the arbitrator and the party, or the affiliate of the party, have no ongoing relationship. 3.1.2 The arbitrator has, within the past three years, served as counsel against one of the parties, or an affiliate of one of the parties, in an unrelated matter. 3.1.3 The arbitrator has, within the past three years, been appointed as arbitrator on two or more occasions by one of the parties, or an affiliate of one of the parties. 3.1.4 The arbitrator's law firm has, within the past three years, acted for or against one of the parties, or an affiliate of one of the parties, in an unrelated matter without the involvement of the arbitrator. 3.1.5 The arbitrator currently serves, or has served within the past three years, as arbitrator in another arbitration on a related issue involving one of the parties, or an affiliate of one of the parties.
3.2 Current services for one of the parties 3.2.1 The arbitrator's law firm is currently rendering services to one of the parties, or to an affiliate of one of the parties, without creating a significant commercial relationship for the law firm and without the involvement of the arbitrator. 3.2.2 A law firm or other legal organisation [sic] that shares significant fees or other revenues with the arbitrator's law firm renders services to one of the parties, or an affiliate of one of the parties, before the Arbitral Tribunal. 3.2.3 The arbitrator or his or her firm represents a party, or an affiliate of one of the parties to the arbitration, on a regular basis, but such representation does not concern the current dispute.

3.3 Relationship between an arbitrator and another arbitrator or counsel 3.3.1 The arbitrator and another arbitrator are lawyers in the same law firm. 3.3.2 The arbitrator and another arbitrator, or the counsel for one of the parties, are members of the same barristers' chambers. 3.3.3 The arbitrator was, within the past three years, a partner of, or otherwise affiliated with, another arbitrator or any of the counsel in the arbitration. 3.3.4 A lawyer in the arbitrator's law firm is an arbitrator in another dispute involving the same party or parties, or an affiliate of one of the parties. 3.3.5 A close family member of the arbitrator is a partner or employee of the law firm representing one of the parties, but is not assisting with the dispute. 3.3.6 A close personal friendship exists between an arbitrator and a counsel of a party. 3.3.7 Enmity exists between an arbitrator and counsel appearing in the arbitration. 3.3.8 The arbitrator has, within the past three years, been appointed on more than three occasions by the same counsel, or the same law firm. 3.3.9 The arbitrator and another arbitrator, or counsel for one of the parties in the arbitration, currently act or have acted together within the past three years as co-counsel.
3.4 Relationship between arbitrator and party and others involved in the arbitration 3.4.1 The arbitrator's law firm is currently acting adversely to one of the parties, or an affiliate of one of the parties. 3.4.2 The arbitrator has been associated with a party, or an affiliate of one of the parties, in a professional capacity, such as a former employee or partner. 3.4.3 A close personal friendship exists between an arbitrator and a manager or director or a member of the supervisory board of: a party; an entity that has a direct economic interest in the award to be rendered in the arbitration; or any person having a controlling influence, such as a controlling shareholder interest, on one of the parties or an affiliate of one of the parties or a witness or expert. 3.4.4 Enmity exists between an arbitrator and a manager or director or a member of the supervisory board of: a party; an entity that has a direct economic interest in the award; or any person having a controlling influence in one of the parties or an affiliate of one of the parties or a witness or expert. 3.4.5 If the arbitrator is a former judge, he or she has, within the past three years, heard a significant case involving one of the parties, or an affiliate of one of the parties.

3.5 Other circumstances 3.5.1 The arbitrator holds shares, either directly or indirectly, that by reason of number or denomination constitute a material holding in one of the parties, or an affiliate of one of the parties, this party or affiliate being publicly listed. 3.5.2 The arbitrator has publicly advocated a position on the case, whether in a published paper, or speech, or otherwise. 3.5.3 The arbitrator holds a position with the appointing authority with respect to the dispute. 3.5.4 The arbitrator is a manager, director or member of the supervisory board, or has a controlling influence on an affiliate of one of the parties, where the affiliate is not directly involved in the matters in dispute in the arbitration.

4. Green List

4.1 Previously expressed legal opinions 4.1.1 The arbitrator has previously expressed a legal opinion (such as in a law review article or public lecture) concerning an issue that also arises in the arbitration (but this opinion is not focused on the case).
4.2 Current services for one of the parties 4.2.1 A firm, in association or in alliance with the arbitrator's law firm, but that does not share significant fees or other revenues with the arbitrator's law firm, renders services to one of the parties, or an affiliate of one of the parties, in an unrelated matter.
4.3 Contacts with another arbitrator, or with counsel for one of the parties 4.3.1 The arbitrator has a relationship with another arbitrator, or with the counsel for one of the parties, through membership in the same professional association, or social or charitable organisation [sic], or through a social media network. 4.3.2 The arbitrator and counsel for one of the parties have previously served together as arbitrators. 4.3.3 The arbitrator teaches in the same faculty or school as another arbitrator or counsel to one of the parties, or serves as an officer of a professional association or social or charitable organisation [sic] with another arbitrator or counsel for one of the parties. 4.3.4 The arbitrator was a speaker, moderator or organiser [sic] in one or more conferences, or participated in seminars or working parties of a professional, social or charitable organisation [sic], with another arbitrator or counsel to the parties.

4.4 Contacts between the arbitrator and one of the parties

4.4.1 The arbitrator has had an initial contact with a party, or an affiliate of a party (or their counsel) prior to appointment, if this contact is limited to the arbitrator's availability and qualifications to serve, or to the names of possible candidates for a chairperson, and did not address the merits or procedural aspects of the dispute, other than to provide the arbitrator with a basic understanding of the case.

4.4.2 The arbitrator holds an insignificant amount of shares in one of the parties, or an affiliate of one of the parties, which is publicly listed.

4.4.3 The arbitrator and a manager, director or member of the supervisory board, or any person having a controlling influence on one of the parties, or an affiliate of one of the parties, have worked together as joint experts, or in another professional capacity, including as arbitrators in the same case.

4.4.4 The arbitrator has a relationship with one of the parties or its affiliates through a social media network.

When to Challenge an Arbitrator

So, an arbitrator discloses a connection, or worse yet, you discover an unsavory relation that calls their impartiality into question. You now know this can be basis for their removal or the overturning of their award, but when should you raise this issue?

The rule of thumb is simple: raise the issue as soon as you become aware of this information. While this may not be enough to stop an arbitration in its tracks, it is worth bringing up the issue if only to record a party's protest. For example, in *Savers v. National Union*, the Sixth Circuit held that the lower court could not halt an arbitration, despite what appeared to be evident partiality from the arbitrators.[6]

Similarly, courts have also ruled parties that actively sit on objectionable information for too long can waive their right to protest all together. Take *Martin v. NTT Data*; there, a petitioner was able to show evident partiality but waited over two months to raise an objection

6. Savers Prop. & Cas. Ins. Co. v. Nat'l Union Fire Ins. Co., 748 F.3d 708, 711 (6th Cir. 2014).

after the disclosure was made.[7] The court held that she had waived her right to object.

But what happens when parties were not aware of the incriminating information? Then, courts say, it all comes down to constructive notice. Did the party know of the arbitrator's background? And if a party didn't know, would reasonable due diligence have brought the conflict to light earlier than it did? In *Monster Energy v. City Bevs. LLC*, the Ninth Circuit found that the objecting party lacked the requisite constructive notice for them to waive their right to object.[8] There, the arbitrator had provided general disclosures at the outset of the arbitration but otherwise failed to note his ownership interest in JAMS, the institution holding the arbitration. Monster Energy had been a repeat client of JAMS, administering 97 of their arbitrations over the course of five years. The court vacated the arbitration award. All of this is to say that parties should us their common sense; when in doubt, raise the issue.

7. Martin v. NTT Data, Inc., No. 20-CV-0686, 2020 U.S. Dist. LEXIS 109490 (E.D. Pa. June 23, 2020).

8. Monster Energy Co. v. City Bevs., LLC, 940 F.3d 1130, 1132 (9th Cir. 2019).

CHAPTER 6

Virtual Hearings

As with many other aspects of contemporary business and legal practice, arbitration appears to have been permanently influenced by the initially forced move to virtual proceedings during the COVID epidemic. In the same way that people may not ever return to their offices to the same degree as they did pre-COVID, arbitration hearings may never again be as in-person as they were a decade ago.

The question for the practitioner is, "What choice do you have?" Based on the case law that has emerged since COVID, the answer is, "Very little unless the agreement expressly provides for a live hearing." To the extent that the arbitration agreement does not specify a live hearing, the issue is entirely within the arbitrator's discretion. Parties challenging that discretion must prove that the arbitrator's decision "substantially prejudiced" their right to due process for courts to consider vacatur.[1]

---

1. *See, e.g.*, Alexander v. Davis Hotel Capital, 178 N.E.3d 827 (Ind. Ct. App. 2021) (While the contract did not specify that hearings be virtual or in-person, respondent claims that the arbitration award must be set aside because the arbitrator conducted a virtual hearing, refused to postpone the hearing, and improperly prevented it from presenting relevant and material evidence. The court found no reason to vacate, because parties fully briefed the matters for hearing and presented relevant witnesses and written testimony in support of their respective positions.); *see also* Gross v. Macphail, 2021 Cal. Super. LEXIS 48098, at *7 (Petitioner argued that she never agreed to a virtual hearing and that she should not have been required to purchase a new computer and learn to operate Zoom, noting that requiring her to do so "place[d] an authorized, unfair, and unjustified burden on [her] of both money and time." The court held that the arbitrator had wide discretion to determine the format of hearings, and she proved neither the abuse of discretion nor prejudice burdens required for vacatur.).

In the presence of extenuating circumstances, such as COVID restrictions, courts have even overridden the parties' contracts implying in-person hearing requirements.[2] In *Dirs. Guild of Am. v. Go2 Z 3*, the court found an arbitrator's decision to hold a remote hearing was not an abuse of discretion, even though the arbitration agreement specifically stated that arbitrations were to be held in Los Angeles at the claimant's offices based on availability. Specifically, the court mused:

> The cited clause does not mandate Respondents' offices or another physical location as an alternative site. Moreover, the agreement states that "[a]ny dispute as to where the arbitration should be held shall be determined by an Arbitrator in Los Angeles selected according to the method set forth herein." Here, the arbitrator determined that the hearing would take place remotely due to COVID safety. During communications in August 2020, the arbitrator stated that he would not conduct in-person hearings for the remainder of 2020 and "possibly well into 2021." When a dispute arose prior the March 25, 2021 hearing, the arbitrator corresponded with Respondents via email. Finding that the parties had never before objected to appearing remotely, the arbitrator ruled that the hearing would proceed as scheduled . . . .
>
> The arbitrator was within his discretion to make this ruling given the authority provided by the arbitration agreement. Remote hearings have become the norm throughout the pandemic, and the Superior Court holds its own law and motion hearings telephonically through LACourtConnect. Beyond the conclusory statement that cross-examination is "difficult if not impossible to do remotely," Respondents present no argument or explanation as to how they would have been prejudiced by a remote hearing in this particular case.[3]

2. *See, e.g.*, Dirs. Guild of Am. v. Go2 Z 3, 2022 Cal. Super. LEXIS 18567, at *2–4 (finding that an arbitrator's decision to hold a remote hearing, even when the agreement implied an in-person hearing, did not compel vacatur of the award, finding that the arbitrator "was within his discretion to make this ruling given the authority provided by the arbitration agreement").

3. *Id.*

Moreover, most institutions have codified this point and amended their rules to make clear that the location of the hearing is a matter for the arbitrator. Take, for example, the following institutional rules.

Rule 32 of the AAA Commercial Arbitration Rules and Mediation Procedures:

> When deemed appropriate, the arbitrator may . . . allow for the presentation of evidence by alternative means including video conferencing, internet communication, telephonic conferences and means other than an in-person presentation. Such alternative means must afford a full opportunity for all parties to present any evidence that the arbitrator deems material and relevant to the resolution of the dispute and, when involving witnesses, provide an opportunity for cross-examination.

JAMS Rule 22(g):

> The Arbitrator has full authority to determine that the Hearing, or any portion thereof, be conducted in person or virtually by conference call, videoconference or using other communications technology with participants in one or more geographical places, or in a combined form. If some or all of the witnesses or other participants are located remotely, the Arbitrator may make such orders and set such procedures as the Arbitrator deems necessary or advisable.

ICC article 26: hearings

> A hearing shall be held if any of the parties so requests or, failing such a request, if the arbitral tribunal on its own motion decides to hear the parties. When a hearing is to be held, the arbitral tribunal, giving reasonable notice, shall summon the parties to appear before it on the day and at the place fixed by it. The arbitral tribunal may decide, after consulting the parties, and on the basis of the relevant facts and circumstances of the case, that any hearing will be conducted by physical attendance or remotely by videoconference, telephone or other appropriate means of communication.

Finally, the courts have made clear that there is no absolute right to a live, in-person hearing, either in the FAA or in the case law.[4] In its 2022 multi-state evaluation, *Does a Right to a Physical Hearing Exist in International Arbitration?*, the International Counsel for Commercial Arbitration asked attorneys whether, given the changes COVID required of each country's arbitration system, parties could still point to an inherent right to an in-person hearing. The answer was no.

> The FAA does not provide the right to a physical hearing. "Neither the Federal Arbitration Act (FAA) nor state laws on international arbitration provides for the right to a physical hearing. . . . While the FAA does not explicitly provide for a right to an arbitration hearing at all, the drafters certainly contemplated that hearings are an integral part of the arbitral process. The FAA is however silent as to how hearings should be conducted, including as to whether any hearing must be physical. This is hardly surprising given that Chapter One of the FAA remains largely as enacted in 1925, when the drafters were unconcerned with the possibility of holding hearings other than in-person. . . ."
>
> 22 states have adopted the Revised Uniform Arbitration Act, drafted by the Uniform Law Commission to promote uniform treatment across jurisdictions. "The RUAA provides that arbitrators may conduct arbitration proceedings as they consider appropriate for a fair and expeditious disposition of the proceeding, limited to parties' agreement, and that failure to postpone a hearing when good cause is shown or to hear material evidence can lead to vacatur. It also provides that 'if an arbitrator orders a hearing, the arbitrator shall set a time and place', a literal reading of which would suggest the tribunal is not obligated to hold a physical hearing."

---

4. Hosking et al., Does a Right to a Physical Hearing Exist in International Arbitration? United States of America (International Counsel for Commercial Arbitration 2022), *available at* https://cdn.arbitration-icca.org/s3fs-public/document/media_document/USA-Right-to-a-Physical-Hearing-Report.pdf.

"U.S. courts have generally held that, absent party agreement to the contrary (either expressly or by reference to arbitration rules), the arbitrators have broad discretion to decide whether or not to hold evidentiary hearings, as well as the format the hearing should take." See Graham v. Scissor-Tail, Inc., 28 Cal. 3d 807, 822 (1981) (finding there was no right to an oral hearing when the by-laws on which the arbitration was based contained a waiver on taking oral testimony and presenting oral arguments); Gary B. BORN, International Commercial Arbitration, 2d ed. (Kluwer Law International 2014) at pp. 2134–35 ("In the United States, the FAA's statutory text is silent regarding procedural matters, but U.S. judicial decisions and other authority uniformly confirm the parties' freedom to agree upon the arbitral procedures, subject only to very limited requirements of procedural fairness.") and p. 2148 (stating that in the U.S. "arbitrators possess broad powers to determine arbitral procedures, absent agreement on such matters by the parties" and citing cases) See, adopting seemingly an opposite opinion, Restatement (Third) U.S. Law Int'l Comm. Arb., §4.19, Reporters' Notes, Comment c, Proposed Final Draft (2019).[5]

Q: To the extent that a right to a physical *hearing in arbitration is not mandatory or does not exist in your jurisdiction, could the arbitral tribunal decide to hold a remote hearing even if the parties had agreed to a physical hearing? What would be the legal consequences of such an order?*

A: "The U.S. Supreme Court has consistently ruled that "arbitration is a matter of contract" and arbitration agreements must be enforced according to their terms. That is so even if the contractual terms lead to inefficient proceedings. This is true whether the agreement at issue involves substantive or procedural matters. Therefore, if the arbitration agreement

5. *Id.*

> requires a physical hearing, either expressly or by reference to arbitration rules, an arbitral tribunal could not order a remote hearing contradicting the parties' agreement. An order under such circumstances could well lead to vacatur for excess of authority. That is so, however, only if the arbitration agreement makes clear the parties' intent to have a physical hearing in any circumstances. U.S. courts apply vacatur provisions narrowly and will not review the arbitrator's construction of the contract except in exceptional circumstances. If the arbitration agreement is silent or ambiguous on whether a hearing will be physically held, the arbitral tribunal has discretion to determine to hold one remotely. The tribunal's decision on whether to hold a hearing or not and its conduct during the hearing will generally be respected, unless it was fundamentally unfair."

This is not surprising given the traditional view that arbitration should be efficient and the more recent realization that many legal proceedings can proceed virtually without adverse impact. Persons who may not ever have contemplated a "virtual" deposition with dozens of exhibits and a witness in a remote hearing room suddenly found themselves skilled at so doing during 2020 and 2021, and those practices will continue across litigation. Where these depositions—or motions or even trial-like merits hearings—take place in arbitration, the policy reasons are all the more in favor of allowing the parties to sit in their home or office in front of their computer screen rather than fly, drive, or travel by train to a remote location. What was once unusual has become the norm, or at least an accepted practice.

This does not mean that all arbitrations have become virtual—far from it. Merits hearings in particular will likely be live absent strong objection. But it does mean that here as elsewhere, the practitioner should be aware of two points stressed throughout this book: the power of the arbitration clause and the perhaps more hidden power of the institutional arbitration clause. As to the former, we stress again: unless you provide expressly for a "live" proceeding, the arbitrator can vary the manner in which the hearing is held, including the ultimate "merits" hearing. As to the latter, be aware that once you choose ABA or JAMS (or most other institutional) arbitration, you are again ceding power to the arbitrator to make this choice.

A Note on Remote Testimony and Third Parties

As Chapter 8 will discuss in more depth, the compelling of remote third-party testimony in arbitration is a complicated subject. FAA section 7, which governs third-party testimony in arbitration, contains language requiring third parties to "appear before" the arbitrator in order to provide evidence. As a result, most circuits agree that because virtual hearings do not place the parties in the physical presence of an arbitrator as originally intended when the statute was written in 1925, district judges cannot compel third parties to comply with arbitrator subpoenas, even where it would be efficient to do so.[6] This is starkly contracted with the arbitrator's general right to override the parties' desire for in-person hearings. This contrast is generally explained by the fact that third parties did not sign the agreement to arbitrate, and did not agree to give the arbitrator power over their testimony, whereas parties to the arbitration did sign over the arbitrator this power.

Some parties argue that courts should be able to compel third-party testimony in arbitration just the same, because the inability to compel virtual third-party depositions costs parties great time and expense. On the flip side, others argue that if the testimony is not worth the time and expense, third parties should not be inconvenienced at all. None of this is to say, however, that a third party cannot voluntarily testify virtually. If a third party agrees to testify, the need to compel testimony disappears.

6. Managed Care Advisory Grp. v. CIGNA Healthcare, 939 F.3d 1145 (11th Cir. 2019).

CHAPTER 7

Discovery in Arbitration

The highest cost ticket item in litigation is often a primary reason for parties to choose arbitration: discovery. Most cases, as we know, settle before trial. That usually means that the bulk of any client's budget, especially in complex disputes, is devoted to the exchange and ferreting out of information—what lawyers, and the rules of procedure in our state and federal courts, call discovery. In recent years, with the advent of electronically stored information (ESI), discovery has become even more robust. Parties now spend substantial resources fighting not about the contents of documents but, as a preliminary round to that, about the mode of discovery, what search terms will be used, the extent to which the search must include texts, and other features of modern communication. Lawyers' thirst for information is boundless. Their clients' budgets, however, might not always be as expansive.

Into this gap comes arbitration. Not always, to be sure, as we will review below. Arbitration and discovery are not mutually exclusive. But arbitration does offer a choice. As with many other features of dispute resolution, such as choice of law, choice of forum, length of the case, and arbitrator experience, arbitration lets lawyers and parties regulate that which in court litigation is totally prescriptive. You have a choice.

Here we come to a myth. Discovery can, and more frequently than not *does*, exist in arbitration. This is a fact that is to some degree generational. Fifty years ago, discovery was less common in arbitration than it is today. The issue was more absolute: choose arbitration and the parties would frequently show up at a hearing with their own documents and witnesses but with no idea of what the other side would produce or what their witnesses would say.

Today, that stark dichotomy is less present. Once parties relinquish their right to litigation and agree to provide an arbitrator with a mandate, the Federal Rules of Evidence and Civil Procedure, with their heavy pro-discovery bias, do not apply. From there, the parties have a choice. They can do the following:

1. Provide expressly in their dispute resolution clause, or in any post-dispute agreement, that there be no discovery at all (admittedly an uncommon result, again especially in complex disputes, but entirely legitimate and consistent with the principle of "party autonomy" that governs arbitration);
2. Regulate discovery heavily from the start in their arbitration clause (for example, by prohibiting or setting a cap upon the number of depositions, or by excluding all forms of written discovery other than requests for document production);
3. Choose an institutional rule regime that includes discovery procedures (more on this below, as institutional rules can be a hidden discovery trap for the unwary); or
4. Wait for the procedural conference, advocate at that conference for their preferred discovery then, and follow the resulting procedural order.

There are pros and cons to each approach.

The Arbitration Clause

As you've already seen, an arbitration clause can be customized to tackle almost any procedural problem a party can foresee arising down the line. Discovery is no different. Parties can, should they so choose, prohibit any and all discovery outright. They can also write their own ad hoc discovery process into the arbitration clause. For example, some drafters prefer to write limited discovery into the arbitration clause itself. Some have even included the Federal Rules of Civil Procedure (FRCP). By adding the FRCP, parties might limit uncertainty as to what disclosures might look like. The downside, however, is that the incorporation of the FRCP eliminates the hallmark efficiency of arbitration—the lack of inlaid litigation rules and the oftentimes ample time and effort required to comply with them. Or, parties can adopt institutional rules (for example, that this arbitration will be governed under the rules of the AAA) and will therefore be governed by that institution's discovery rules.

The advantage of prescribing (and in some cases proscribing) discovery procedures in the arbitration clause is certainty. That certainty, however, comes with the disadvantage of ignorance, which the authors hasten to stress is not used here pejoratively. Ignorance is a fact. We generally know very little about a case on its first day, or after a client leaves our office or hangs up from that first call. At best—assuming full and candid disclosure by our client and immediate comprehension on the lawyer's part—we know one side of the story. That ignorance is many times magnified at the time the parties negotiate their commercial agreement with the dispute resolution clause, because at that point there is no dispute at all. There is, in fact, completely the opposite: two parties who wish to come together on a commercial transaction (or employment agreement or other such relationship). The parties are in a marriage, not a divorce. How, then, can counsel who negotiate the dispute resolution clause, which calls for arbitration, know what discovery tactics they need if the relationship turns stormy?

Our advice here, then, is to preserve flexibility. We have seen too many arbitration clauses by which arbitration is overregulated. Parties then need to backtrack, but may not be able to do so if their opponents dig in and/or the arbitrator is stubborn. It is better then to anticipate some discovery but provide that it shall be in some form limited by the conference, by rules, or by agreement of the parties. Here as always, party autonomy should govern. Use that as a weapon and not a hindrance.

It is also advisable, though hardly always possible, to consider at the time of contracting the type of dispute most likely to arise between the parties and thus the type, and extent, of discovery best suited to the client's position in that dispute. If, for example, the client is a seller of goods and the dispute is likely to be over payment, does your client really need to discover all that much besides payment? But if you are representing the buyer, then you might want to discover all kinds of information about shoddy manufacturing and cost cutting as support for your potential case one day in which you advance excuses for nonpayment. Consider as well who owns the intellectual property (IP) in a particular contract and how that consideration may enter into the discovery parameters you wish to adopt. Your client may want IP to be freely discovered or heavily regulated. Much of this is hard to know in advance—we rarely know which way disputes will break. But as you hammer out a dispute resolution clause and come to the discovery portions of that section, it is worth at least considering what you may want and when. This is another feature of "building your own courthouse."

Institutional Rules

Institutional rules are increasingly used in modern arbitration, especially by commercial actors. *Modern institutional rules allow for discovery.* This is a critical point of advice to your clients. Picking arbitration with institutional rules does not foreclose discovery. Quite to the contrary, picking institutional arbitration guarantees discovery. Most rules provide the arbitrator wide authority to control the exchange of information

Each institution's rules on discovery are different. We summarize these here.

JAMS Rule 17. Exchange of Information

(a) The Parties shall cooperate in good faith in the voluntary and informal exchange of all non-privileged documents and other information (including electronically stored information ("ESI")) relevant to the dispute or claim immediately after commencement of the Arbitration. They shall complete an initial exchange of all relevant, non-privileged documents, including, without limitation, copies of all documents in their possession or control on which they rely in support of their positions, and names of individuals whom they may call as witnesses at the Arbitration Hearing, within twenty-one (21) calendar days after all pleadings or notice of claims have been received. The Arbitrator may modify these obligations at the Preliminary Conference.

(b) Each Party may take one deposition of an opposing Party or of one individual under the control of the opposing Party. The Parties shall attempt to agree on the time, location and duration of the deposition. If the Parties do not agree, these issues shall be determined by the Arbitrator. The necessity of additional depositions shall be determined by the Arbitrator based upon the reasonable need for the requested information, the availability of other discovery options and the burdensomeness of the request on the opposing Parties and the witness.

(c) As they become aware of new documents or information, including experts who may be called upon to testify, all Parties continue to be obligated to provide relevant, non-privileged documents to supplement their identification of witnesses and experts and to honor any informal agreements or understandings between the Parties regarding documents or information to be exchanged. Documents that were not previously exchanged, or witnesses and experts that were not previously identified, may not be considered by the Arbitrator at the Hearing, unless agreed by the Parties or upon a showing of good cause.

(d) The Parties shall promptly notify JAMS when a dispute exists regarding discovery issues. A conference shall be arranged with the Arbitrator, either by telephone or in person, and the Arbitrator shall decide the dispute. With the written consent of all Parties, and in accordance with an agreed written procedure, the Arbitrator may appoint a special master to assist in resolving a discovery dispute.

(e) In a consumer or employment case, the Parties may take discovery of third parties with the approval of the Arbitrator.

The JAMS rules explicitly include provisions governing the production of electrically stored information. Consider whether your client might appreciate a provision like this or would rather avoid the time and cost that comes with electronic document recovery and organization. JAMS also provides for only one deposition of the opposing party, leaving additional depositions to the judgment of an arbitrator. The AAA rules, on the other hand, start out with basic self-executing disclosures but leave the rest up to the arbitrator.

At the far end of the spectrum, the ICC rules leave everything to the arbitrator.

ICC Article 25: Establishing the Facts of the Case

1. The arbitral tribunal shall proceed within as short a time as possible to establish the facts of the case by all appropriate means.
2. The arbitral tribunal may decide to hear witnesses, experts appointed by the parties or any other person, in the presence of the parties, or in their absence provided they have been duly summoned.
3. The arbitral tribunal, after consulting the parties, may appoint one or more experts, define their terms of reference and receive their reports. At the request of a party, the parties shall be given the opportunity to question at a hearing any such expert.
4. At any time during the proceedings, the arbitral tribunal may summon any party to provide additional evidence.
5. The arbitral tribunal may decide the case solely on the documents submitted by the parties unless any of the parties requests a hearing.

The AAA falls into the middle of the spectrum by providing guidance to arbitrators on how to exercise their discretion.

AAA Rule 22. Pre-Hearing Exchange and Production of Information

(a) Authority of arbitrator. The arbitrator shall manage any necessary exchange of information among the parties with a view to achieving an efficient and economical resolution of the dispute, while at the same time promoting equality of treatment and safeguarding each party's opportunity to fairly present its claims and defenses.

(b) Documents. The arbitrator may, on application of a party or on the arbitrator's own initiative:

i. require the parties to exchange documents in their possession or custody on which they intend to rely;

ii. require the parties to update their exchanges of the documents on which they intend to rely as such documents become known to them;

iii. require the parties, in response to reasonable document requests, to make available to the other party documents, in the responding party's possession or custody, not otherwise readily available to the party seeking the documents, reasonably believed by the party seeking the documents to exist and to be relevant and material to the outcome of disputed issues; and

iv. require the parties, when documents to be exchanged or produced are maintained in electronic form, to make such documents available in the form most convenient and economical for the party in possession of such documents, unless the arbitrator determines that there is good cause for requiring the documents to be produced in a different form. The parties should attempt to agree in advance upon, and the arbitrator may determine, reasonable search parameters to balance the need for production of electronically stored documents relevant and material to the outcome of disputed issues against the cost of locating and producing them.

Procedural Orders

In more complex arbitrations, the majority of guidance regarding discovery procedures will come in the form of a procedural order. Arbitrators issue procedural orders in the early stages of a case. These orders set the schedule and tone for the rest of the process, and they often include the types of discovery parties are expected to produce. Parties also have a hand in shaping these orders during the prehearing conference. The below is an example of what one might expect to see in a procedural order:

International Centre for Dispute Resolution

In the matter of the Arbitration between

Claimant	:	
	:	
And	:	Case No.
	:	
Respondent	:	

FIRST PROCEDURAL ORDER

Preliminary hearing teleconferences were held on ______________ commencing at approximately ______________ before Arbitrator __________. Collectively appearing at the teleconferences were ______________________ and- all Counsel for Claimant; __________, and ______________ all Counsel for Respondent; and (hereinafter, all counsel for the parties are collectively referred to as simply "Counsel" except where the context specifically indicates otherwise).

A. As a result of the teleconferences:
   1. Neither the Arbitrator nor Counsel had any further disclosures for the other.

2. The following schedule, to which Counsel have mutually agreed, is now in effect (all deadlines are on the date indicated):
   (a) By ___________, All discovery will close.
   (b) By ___________, Each side will identify its experts to the other. Expert reports are to be exchanged.
   (c) By ___________, Rebuttal expert reports are to be exchanged.
   (d) By ___________, Counsel will exchange witness lists.
   (e) By ___________, Counsel will exchange supplemental witness lists and exhibits.
3. By _________, Pre-hearing briefs are to be exchanged and filed with the Arbitration The Evidentiary (Arbitration) Hearing will take place in and start on ______and continue on successive days through ______, if necessary.

   The parties will decide later what specific facility to use for the hearing based on seating capacity and/or other salient factors. This and all other hearing-related issues (e.g., obtaining a stenographic record, and the type of award requested—bald, partially reasoned, fully reasoned) will all be appropriately addressed by Counsel and the Arbitrator at a subsequent teleconference.

B. Further Aspects

4. Counsel will use the "direct exchange" program, as offered by the AAA and ICDR, under which Counsel may send all their submissions directly to the Arbitrator by e-mail (and/or by Courier where necessary for shipments of electronic media), provided the submitting Counsel copies both Counsel for the other side and the ICDR on each such submission then being sent.
5. The Panel adopts the attached PROCEDURAL CHECKLIST which will govern: submissions to the Panel, hearing exhibits, hearing testimony and transcripts. The Panel welcomes any suggestion which Counsel may have to any

item set forth in the CHECKLIST in the interest of simplifying the proceeding or Counsels' efforts, or increasing the efficiency of the proceeding.

6. Several discovery disputes currently exist between Counsel, including, e.g., a limit on the number of depositions to be taken by each side; what categories of documents should be searched by each side, including whether and to what extent electronically stored information is to be included in any such search; and a schedule of document production. To quickly resolve these and other discovery disputes, the Arbitrator has suggested and Counsel has agreed to the following:
   (a) By ___________, Counsel for each side will serve their document requests on the other;
   (b) Later during the week of ___________ and extending through April 1, 20__, Counsel will meet and confer, in light of their requests, in an effort to resolve their existing discovery disputes and, in view of the discovery cutoff, attempt to anticipate whatever future discovery disputes might otherwise arise and reach suitable agreements to avoid them; and
   (c) On ___________ at ___________ and through facilities provided by the ICDR, a teleconference will occur with Counsel and the Arbitrator to:
      (i) address all these disputes, including the resolutions reached by Counsel; and
      (ii) present to the Arbitrator for resolution all unresolved discovery disputes then remaining.

   Further procedural and logistical aspects of the proceeding, including additional periodic status teleconferences and a pre-hearing teleconference, will also be discussed with the Arbitrator during the April 2nd teleconference.

7. Motions

   In the event either party desires to file a motion during this proceeding, Counsel for that party will first submit to the Arbitrator a brief letter memo (not to exceed approximately three pages):

(a) requesting permission to file the motion;

(b) explaining the nature of the requested motion;

(c) explaining why the motion is necessary, particularly addressing any beneficial effect the motion, if granted, will likely have on the proceeding; and

(d) explaining why the Arbitrator is more likely than not to grant the motion.

The non-requesting party will then have five working days, from the date on which the requesting party filed its supporting memo, to file its own letter memo, also not to exceed approximately three pages, providing its response. The pendency of any request to file a motion, absent a procedural ruling by the Arbitrator, will not stay any aspect of this proceeding or modify any existing due dates. Motions are only to be filed with the approval of the Arbitrator and in accordance with a briefing schedule established by the Arbitrator and the parties.

8. This arbitration shall be governed by the Commercial Arbitration Rules (amended and effective June 1, 2009) as referenced in ___________ of the _______ signed by the parties and dated _______ 20__.

   All provisions of this order shall remain in effect unless and until amended by a subsequent order of the Arbitrator.

SO ORDERED.
(ICDR case number:)

It is important to note that these three bases for discovery need not be applied in isolation from one another; a clause might stipulate to a certain type of discovery outright and select an institutional rule regime with discovery rules. These rules and the clause likely give the arbitrator power to order discovery; where this is the case, parties should arrive to the prehearing conference prepared to discuss the type of discovery they want to see and the schedule on which it should be produced. In this way parties can proactively take charge of discovery and make use of the unique ability arbitration affords to create their own disclosures process, often at a much quicker pace than litigation.

Electronic Discovery

Electronic discovery is increasingly the dominant mode of discovery today. Arbitration is no different from litigation in adopting Electronic Discovery Services EDS protocols and procedures. Most institutional rules either permit or go so far as to require electronic discovery. It is therefore critical that clients be advised that (1) picking arbitration but then picking institutional rules to govern that arbitration does NOT get them out of discovery obligations imposed by EDS, and in fact, directly to the contrary: they have bought directly into EDS, *and* (2) in any event they are going to wind up in discovery whether or not they arbitrate, so they should consider in advance what kind of case they are most likely to have in arbitration.

That said, arbitration is nothing if not customizable, and parties do have the choice to place EDS limits directly into their governing clause. Parties might consider limiting a production to a certain number of document custodians or search terms each side can request of the other. Pause to consider your client's needs and the context of a possible dispute. Budget is one consideration. Is your client a small shop with a tight bottom line? Are they a large company with large swaths of potentially discoverable information likely to make for an expensive production? Are you contracting for a relatively simple sale or service? In these cases, you may want to consider placing EDS parameters to limit the time, money, and sheer effort required by production. Size variables might be a second consideration. Is your client a well-organized individual or smaller company contracting with a larger company? Do you foresee an information imbalance between the parties? Perhaps you would prefer not to place EDS limits, as your electronic database is easily produced and you prefer not to limit your requests on your opposing party.

CHAPTER 8

Third-Party Evidence

Third-party discovery in arbitration is a thorny and unresolved issue. The key question is "where": where is the witness, where are the documents, and where is your arbitration? From there we get to unsettled questions and a genuine circuit split. The skilled practitioner in a case that requires third-party evidence will attempt to control for this split.

You've just seen how, with the right drafting and rule choice, parties can harness the power of discovery in arbitration to make their dispute resolution process faster, cheaper, and more efficient than it would be in court. Party discovery in arbitration no doubt has the potential—in fact, the base-level engineering—to make fewer problems for those participating. Rather than proceed from a given template of procedural rules as in litigation, parties can combine the rules of the arbitral institution (if any) governing their particular action with any further understandings they reach with opposing counsel *and* with any particular orders entered by the arbitrator, all done in a manner to minimize discovery disputes and make arbitration more efficient.

This is true enough for party discovery. It is much less true in cases of third-party evidence. The rules on discovery from third parties are a confusing and geographically inconsistent muddle. Understanding that muddle and how to play what step where is another area where understanding a complicated part of arbitration will put any practitioner at a key advantage.

What Makes Third-Party Discovery in Arbitration Different?

Third-party evidence is often critical irrespective of the form of the dispute resolution proceeding. The third-party witness frequently has no "skin in the game"—that is, no financial or other interest in the outcome—and so may often be perceived by the finder of fact as the most credible witness (and source of documentary evidence).

In federal courts, FRCP Rule 45 governs this all-important process. In state courts, most states have codified some version of this rule alongside the Uniform Interstate Depositions and Discovery Act, which standardizes the enforcement cross-state of subpoenas. A litigating party can therefore subpoena, serve, depose, and call to trial almost any third party possessing relevant evidence in a case.

Access to third-party evidence is more difficult in arbitration, at least in the discovery process. Section 7 of the FAA governs third-party evidence. It provides:

> The arbitrators selected either as prescribed in this title or otherwise, or a majority of them, *may summon in writing any person to attend before them* or any of them as a witness and in a proper case to bring with him or them any book, record, document, or paper which may be deemed material as evidence in the case. [. . .] Said summons shall issue in the name of the arbitrator or arbitrators, or a majority of them, and shall be signed by the arbitrators, or a majority of them, and shall be directed to the said person and shall be served in the same manner as subpoenas to appear and testify before the court; if any person or persons so summoned to testify shall refuse or neglect to obey said summons, upon petition the United States district court for the district in which such arbitrators, or a majority of them, are sitting may compel the attendance

> of such person or persons before said arbitrator or arbitrators, or punish said person or persons for contempt in the same manner provided by law for securing the attendance of witnesses or their punishment for neglect or refusal to attend in the courts of the United States.[1]

(emphasis added).

The issue is the "appear before them" language italicized above. The language makes clear that arbitrators have broad discretion (and jurisdiction) over third parties to compel their persons, and their documents, to attend the actual arbitration hearing. But what about prehearing discovery? The answer is far less clear. Courts generally disagree as to *when* this third-party discovery might be taken and *where* exactly the territorial reach of an arbitral subpoena extends. It is thus critically important in sophisticated arbitration practice involving third-party evidence to know where you are playing and under what rules.

In short, there are two main questions to ask when evaluating your ability to participate in arbitral third-party prehearing discovery:

1. Does the jurisdiction in which the witness resides allow third-party prehearing discovery in arbitration?
2. Does the jurisdiction in which the witness resides enforce subpoenas from arbitrations seated in your location?

When: Does the FAA Allow Third-Party Prehearing Discovery?

Section 7 places third-party discovery decisions squarely in the hands of the arbitrators. This includes the taking of depositions, production of documents, and compelling of attendance—a large departure from the general "hands-off" nature of evidence gathering in litigation. According to this section, arbitrators may summon a third party "to attend before them" as a witness. But what does this mean, exactly? Does it mean that the arbitrator must be present at every deposition? And does this mean that third-party discovery can be taken only at

1. 9 U.S.C. § 7: Witnesses before arbitrators; fees; compelling attendance.

a hearing (arbitration's trial-equivalent)? Or is prehearing discovery available?

As noted above, courts disagree. The Sixth and Eighth Circuits read the statute to necessarily imply the incorporation of nonparty prehearing discovery in the arbitrator's discovery repertoire.[2] In holding that arbitrators can subpoena third parties for prehearing discovery, these courts reason that all prehearing discovery, both party based and nonparty based, furthers the efficient resolution of arbitral disputes. Just as in litigation, these circuits will therefore enforce subpoenas issued by an arbitrator requiring the production of third-party evidence prior to the arbitral hearing. Parties can conduct this discovery outside the presence of an arbitrator.

The Second, Third, and Ninth Circuits, on the other hand, interpret this language quite literally: section 7 requires that the nonparty come before the arbitrator to provide documents and oral testimony. In *Hay Group Inc. v. E.B.S. Acquisition Corp.*, then-Judge Alito highlighted this word-by-word evaluation:

> The power to require a non-party "to bring" items "with him" clearly applies only to situations in which the non-party accompanies the items to the arbitration proceeding, not to situations in which the items are simply sent or brought by a courier. In addition, the use of the word "and" makes it clear that a non-party may be compelled "to bring" items "with him" only when [. . .] summoned "to attend before [the arbitrator] as a witness." Thus, Section 7's language unambiguously restricts an arbitrator's subpoena power to situations in which the non-party has been called to appear in the physical presence of the arbitrator and to hand over the documents at this time.[3]

2. Security Life Ins. Co. of Am. v. Duncanson & Holt Inc., 228 F.3d 865, 870–71 (8th Cir. 2000); *see also* Television and Radio Artists v. WJBK-TV, 164 F.3d 1004, 1010 (6th Cir. 1999).

3. Hay Group Inc. v. E.B.S. Acquisition Corp. 360 F.3d 404 (3d Cir. 2004); *see also* CVS Health Corp. v. Vividus LLC, 878 F.3d 703, 708 (9th Cir. 2017).

These circuits therefore have held that section 7 does not provide arbitrators with prehearing subpoena power, as the nonparties must truly be present "before" them when providing documents or testimony (and the hearing is, to the literalist courts, the only time a nonparty would stand before an arbitrator). These courts will therefore refuse to enforce subpoenas granted by an arbitrator for nonparties to produce documents or testimony prior to a hearing.

There is a third way. A subset of courts soften the blow of strict literalism by allowing for a slightly more time-consuming, yet ingenious, loophole. In his *Hay Group* concurrence, Judge Chertoff notes that the *Hay Group* ruling need not foreclose arbitrating parties from all third-party prehearing discovery. Instead, the judge broached the possibility of a "mini-hearing" prior to the main event, in which arbitrators could subpoena nonparties to come before them expressly for the purpose of presenting evidence. The Second Circuit later provided its seal of approval to this method in *Stolt-Nielsen v. Celanese*.[4] This way, arbitrators can issue a subpoena for a third party to attend a shorter hearing prior to the main hearing; the nonparty could attend before the arbitrator to present their evidence, be it document based or testimony based, and this evidence could be assessed and presented by the parties in their main hearing.[5] Mini-hearings reconcile the literal requirement that an arbitrator be present for the production of nonparty evidence with the practical requirement that parties be able to gather prehearing nonparty discovery in the interest of efficiency.

The Fourth Circuit is an outlier. In *COMSAT Corp. v. Natl. Science Foundation*, the Fourth Circuit put forward an approach in which arbitrators may compel discovery under specific circumstances only.[6] The court agreed with the majority of circuits that section 7 does not provide arbitrators with the power to issue nonparty prehearing discovery

4. Stolt-Nielsen Transp. Grp., Inc. v. Celanese AG, 430 F.3d 567, 577–78 (2d Cir. 2005); *see also* Life Receivables Trust v. Syndicate 102 at Lloyd's London, 549 F.3d 210 (2008).

5. On the plus side, the inconvenience of being required to present before an arbitrator may be enough to make a witness present the documents without being compelled by a court to do so.

6. COMSAT Corp. v. Natl. Science Foundation, 190 F.3d 269, 275 (4th Cir. 1999).

subpoenas, but it also suggested an arbitration panel may be able to garner this power "upon a showing of special need or hardship."[7] While attractive on its face, the Fourth Circuit has provided no real guidance encouraging the real-world application of this theory.[8]

While the arbitration world still lacks a solid answer from the Supreme Court on the matter, one thing is abundantly clear: parties should be aware of the laws of the circuit both in which they are arbitrating and where the witness sits. For third-party discovery, it makes a world of difference.

Here is a quick cheat sheet:

- Circuits that will enforce an arbitrator's third-party prehearing subpoena:
  - Sixth Circuit
  - Eighth Circuit
- Circuits that will NOT enforce an arbitrator's third-party prehearing subpoena:
  - Third Circuit
  - Ninth Circuit
- Circuits that will enforce an arbitrator's third-party prehearing subpoena via "mini-hearing":
  - Second Circuit
  - Eleventh Circuit** (*See discussion of In re Managed Care on page 82, infra*)
- Circuits that will enforce an arbitrator's third-party prehearing subpoena where a party can show special need or hardship:
  - Fourth Circuit
- Undecided:
  - First Circuit

7. *Id.* at 276.

8. *See* Matthew Adler & Benjamin Eichel, *When, Where and Whether: The Confusing Law of Third-Party Evidence*, TROUTMAN PEPPER (Apr. 1, 2019), https://www.troutman.com/insights/when-where-and-whether-the-confusing-law-of-third-party-evidence.html.

Where: How Does Location Restrain an Arbitrator Subpoena?

Assume that you have done the "where" inquiry recommended strongly in this chapter and so have determined that your witness is located in a jurisdiction that will enforce third-party discovery. You issue the subpoena, but the witness refuses to comply. Can you simply ask the presiding court with jurisdiction over your witness to mandate compliance? Unfortunately, it is not this simple. Even if the presiding jurisdiction allows third-party discovery, the location of the arbitration issuing the subpoena also comes into play. Again, the courts are split, and again, the law in the district with jurisdiction over your particular witness (or documents) governs. In an effort do something more useful here than point practitioners in the direction of the nearest case library, this section will examine a sampling of what courts have held thus far.

First, some background. In federal litigation, FRCP Rule 45 expressly requires any district court to issue a subpoena to any witness residing in that district whose testimony is needed for a trial in a different district. This creates nationwide jurisdiction over third-party witnesses. Not so in arbitration. As it so happens, there is uncertainty among courts as to whether an arbitrator's subpoena should be enforced in the seat of the arbitrator or the location of the witness. Section 7 notes that a subpoena may be enforced by the district in which the arbitrator sits—however, because Rule 45 does not apply to arbitration, this would mean that the arbitrator has no power to subpoena anyone outside the district in which they sit.

In *Amgen Inc. v. Kidney Ctr. of Delaware County Ltd.*, the Northern District of Illinois held that it must be possible for parties to obtain evidence located outside of the judicial district in which the arbitration sits.[9] There, an arbitrator sitting in Chicago issued a subpoena to a company in Pennsylvania, but when the parties attempted to enforce the subpoena in Pennsylvania, the court transferred the case back to the Northern District of Illinois—the proper court under section 7. Under traditional rules, the Northern District of Illinois would technically

9. Amgen Inc. v. Kidney Ctr., 879 F. Supp. 878, 882 (N.D. Ill. 1995).

not have jurisdiction over a Pennsylvania company without the help of the Pennsylvania court. The court rejected this theory, however, because "[t]o find that the wording of the FAA precludes issuance and enforcement of an arbitrator's subpoena of a witness outside the district in which he or she sits, particularly where, as here, such discovery is agreed upon by the parties to the arbitration, would likely lead to rejection of arbitration clauses altogether,"—which, if you remember back to Chapter 1, would fly in the face of SCOTUS's liberal federal policy in favor of arbitration.[10] Instead, the *Amgen* court "gap filled," applying the Rule 45 standard that would allow a lawyer to issue a subpoena under the district in which the arbitrator sits and allow the court in the location of the witness to enforce it.

The Second Circuit, on the other hand, expressly rejected this gap-filling technique. In *Dynegy Midstream Servs., LP v. Trammochem,* it held that if the FAA did not explicitly provide arbitrators with a nationwide service of process, then arbitrators were limited in the same manner as if they were sitting their respective district court. This gap filling was clearly not intended, the court held, because section 7 does not allow lawyers to issue subpoenas in arbitration.[11]

The Southern District of Florida agreed. In *In re Managed Care,* that court recognized that the Second Circuit's interpretation created an enforcement gap, "[b]ut it is up to Congress, not a court, to fill such gaps."[12]

True to form, the Eighth Circuit declared itself in favor of arbitration and efficiency. In *Security Life Ins. Co. of Am. v. Duncanson & Holt Inc.*, the court simply held the territoriality argument to be unnecessary: "we do not believe an order for the production of documents requires compliance with Rule 45(b)(2)'s territorial limit."[13]

10. *Id.*; *see also* Moses H. Cone Memorial Hospital v. Mercury Construction Corp., 460 U.S. 1 (1983).

11. Dynegy Midstream Servs. LP v. Trammochem, 451 D.3d 89 (2d Cir. 2006).

12. *In re* Managed Care Litig., No. 00-01334-MD, 1334, 2020 U.S. Dist. LEXIS 117788 (S.D. Fla. July 6, 2020).

13. Security Life Ins. Co. of Am. v. Duncanson & Holt Inc., 228 F.3d 865, 872 (8th Cir. 2000).

Because such uncertainty exists, it is still difficult to split the current decisions by circuit. Some parties have opted to hold a section of the arbitration hearing or mini-hearing in the location where the witness sits, thereby taking advantage of section 7 discovery. Ultimately, in this instance too, parties should be wary of the territoriality requirement when looking to enforce an arbitrator's third-party subpoena.

Practice Tip: Caution—Virtual Hearings Don't Always Satisfy Section 7

In the aftermath of COVID, litigating parties are increasingly moving depositions online. However, in light of the section 7 interpretation explained above, some courts have been less than enthusiastic about allowing virtual hearings for nonparty testimony. In *Managed Care Advisory Grp. v. CIGNA Healthcare*, the Eleventh Circuit agreed with the Second, Third, Fourth, and Ninth Circuits in finding section 7's "appear before" language provided no outright prehearing subpoena power to arbitrators.[14] However, the court went further. In evaluating a subpoena served upon a nonparty requiring a virtual mini-hearing, the court determined that the nonparty's virtual attendance did not satisfy the "appear before" requirement. Because the parties would not be in the physical presence of the arbitrator as originally intended when the statute was written in 1925, the district judge had abused his discretion in requiring the nonparty to comply. The arbitrator had no power to subpoena a party virtually.

While the law on this topic is far from settled (and this would be less of an issue in the Sixth and Eight Circuits where the courts have already determined that an arbitrator must not be present for nonparty discovery), it may still pose an issue for parties arbitrating in a literal interpretation court.

---

14. Managed Care Advisory Grp. v. CIGNA Healthcare, 939 F.3d 1145 (11th Cir. 2019).

CHAPTER 9

Third Parties in Arbitration

Arbitration clauses are bilateral, but not all disputes are bilateral. In litigation, the procedural rules allow for such devices as joinder and impleader, or, less complicated, simply suing multiple defendants at once. But what happens when your client may have an arbitration clause with only one of the parties involved in the dispute? Or what happens when your client has an arbitration clause with one party and a court-based dispute resolution clause with another? Must you engage in piecemeal litigation? Or can you bring in "nonsignatories," that is, a party or parties other than the one who signed the arbitration clause with your client, to the arbitration? From the opposite perspective, what if your client never signed an arbitration agreement but is now being asked—or demanded—to join an arbitration between the signatories because of your client's alleged involvement in the dispute?

We explore those issues in this chapter. The difficulty is in the opening line: if the arbitration agreement is consensual and bilateral, then how does third-party practice get harmonized with the need for "consensus" in arbitration? How do you join someone who by definition has not consented to the arbitration and may have no wish to do so?

You already know that bringing third parties into arbitration in any form necessarily breeds complications. This stems from the fact, as does all arbitration law, that arbitration is at bottom a creature of contract. We have introduced the idea that parties can be made to give up their guaranteed right to due process in the interest of efficiency and confidentiality only when they have, at some point, explicitly agreed to do so. So how, you may ask, does this theory apply to the incorporation of third parties who never signed a contract in the first place?

Contract law still governs all dispute resolution. The equitable resolution of contract disputes sometimes necessitates allowing third parties to join (or forcibly attaching them to) an arbitration in which they have a recognized interest in the outcome. As you know from litigation, this can occur when a third party wants to be bound by the outcome of or participate in a case, or when a plaintiff is required to join a party to ensure equitable resolution for those involved.

For practitioners more familiar with litigation, this will come as a relief; to those more versed in arbitration, this turns their consent-based arbitration worldview on its head. Regardless of the side upon which you fall, third-party joinder is an essential skill to understand and apply.

First, a short background history. In 2009, SCOTUS granted cert in *Arthur Andersen v. Carlisle*, a multi-party appeal from the Sixth Circuit arising out of a multi-defendant construction investment dispute. Before trial, one of the defendants moved to stay their section of the litigation under FAA section 3, while that defendant and Carlisle underwent arbitration pursuant to a separate agreement. The Court granted this motion, and several other defendants likewise moved to a stay, reasoning that, despite not being party to the Carlisle arbitration agreement, allowing one party to arbitrate while requiring the others to litigate at the same time would be contradictory. SCOTUS held that third parties may pursue and obtain a stay under FAA section 3 "whenever the relevant state law would make a contract to arbitrate a particular dispute enforceable by a non-signatory."[1]

And in one fell swoop, SCOTUS forged the two major conclusions underlying all third-party incorporation:

1. Arthur Andersen v. Carlisle, 556 U.S. 624 (2009).

1. Nonsignatories can be brought under an arbitration agreement to which they were not an original party, ensuring that nonparties were entitled to relief under arbitration clauses not their own; and
2. This process is dictated by state law.

It is important to remember that no federal law bars a state from allowing petitioners to enforce an arbitration agreement against respondents. The lower courts have recognized that this precedent would also apply to the incorporation of nonparties in an arbitration where a signatory requests their incorporation against the will of the nonparty.[2]

There are five generally accepted bases for third-party incorporation in contract law and therefore in arbitration as well. These are (1) incorporation by reference, (2) assumption, (3) agency, (4) veil piercing/alter ego, and (5) third-party beneficiary/estoppel. While these concepts are generally familiar to most litigators, this chapter will examine how they arise in the context of arbitration. Spot one of these in your own case, and someone (hopefully you) likely has a strong argument for third-party incorporation.

Incorporation by Reference

As in litigation, incorporation by reference is used in arbitration to compel a nonparty to arbitrate where the arbitration agreement, which the nonparty did not sign, is incorporated in a separate contract to which the nonparty is a signatory. Courts here are looking for evidence that the party did agree to arbitrate in some other agreement, and it knew or should have known that the agreement would govern a second. While all states are slightly different, courts generally find incorporation by reference is proper where:

- The underlying contract makes a clear reference to a separate document,
- The identity of that document may be readily ascertained, and

2. *See, e.g.*, NA Rugby Union v. United States Rugby Football League, 442 P.3d 859 (Colo. 2019).

- The incorporation of the document will not result in surprise or hardship to the third party.[3]

As a general rule, broad incorporation language is also sufficient to tie an arbitration clause to another contract. For example, in *Spinks v. Krystal Co.*, the court acknowledged that a guaranty agreement requiring that each party "agrees to be personally bound by . . . each and every provision in the Franchise Agreement" did in fact incorporate an arbitration clause contained in the franchise agreement. That agreement included a clause that maintained:

> [e]xcept as specifically otherwise provided [. . .] any and all disputes and controversies between Krystal and Franchisee and any claim by either party that cannot be amicably settled shall be determined exclusively by arbitration conduced in Hamilton County, Tennessee in accordance with the Uniform Arbitration Act.[4]

Together, the court found that these documents necessarily implied that the party to the guaranty agreement had also adopted the language of the franchise agreement by incorporation.

Signatures are not required on all documents for one to incorporate the other, either; contracts concluded on the same general subject by the same parties can be considered one contract incorporated by reference. Incorporation can also occur when a nonparty enters into a separate contractual relationship with a nonsignatory, and that separate contract incorporates the existing arbitration clause into the signed agreement.

3. *See, e.g.*, Spinks v. Krystal Co, No. 6:07-2619-HMH, 2007 U.S. Dist. LEXIS 94571 (D.S.C. Dec. 20, 2007); *see also* Logan & Kanawha Coal Co., Ltd. Liab. Co. v. Detherage Coal Sales, Ltd. Liab. Co., 514 F. App'x 365, 366 (4th Cir. 2013).

4. *See, e.g.*, Spinks v. Krystal Co, No. 6:07-2619-HMH, 2007 U.S. Dist. LEXIS 94571, at *3 (D.S.C. Dec. 20, 2007).

Assumption

A nonparty may also be bound to an arbitration agreement if their conduct indicates that they have assumed the obligation to arbitrate. This can occur when a nonsignatory assumes the duties or benefits of a party who is subject to an arbitration clause (i.e., as a successor in interest). Some courts may refer to this as a party's manifestation of an "intent to be bound."

Take *Gvozdenovic v. United Air Lines*. There, after United Airlines acquired Pan Am, flight attendant issues were taken to arbitration.[5] Gvozdenovic, a flight attendant who had actively and voluntarily participated in an arbitration to resolve a dispute with United, later reneged on his consent to arbitrate after the arbitrator issued an opposing award. Gvozdenovic argued that he had not signed an agreement to arbitrate, but the court found that "although a party is bound by an arbitral award only where it has agreed to arbitrate, an agreement may be implied from the party's conduct."[6] In short, the classic phrase known to all rings true yet again: provable intent is mightier than the pen.

Agency

In most circumstances, an agent, employee, or representative of a principal is bound to a valid arbitration agreement if the principal is bound to that same agreement. Under the agency theory, a nonparty to an arbitration can be compelled to arbitrate—just like how a real estate agent carrying out duties on behalf of a buyer could bind the buyer to an agreement. However, courts will examine relationships closely, relying on common law agency principles to determine when exactly a nonsignatory is bound by an agent's agreement.

Employee disputes are one such area where this version of incorporation is often applied. Courts widely recognize that when claims

---

5. Gvozdenovic v. United Air Lines, Inc., 933 F.2d 1100 (2d Cir. 1991). *But see* Ouadani v.TF Final Mile LLC, 876 F.3d 31 (1st Cir. 2017).

6. *Gvozdenovic*, 933 F.3d. at 1105.

arise out of conduct by an employee in their capacity as an agent of their employer, that employee is entitled to seek the protection of the employer's arbitration clause.[7] In *Grand Wireless v. Verizon*, for example, the First Circuit found that a Verizon employee could avail herself of the arbitration contract signed between her employer and Grand Wireless after she sent misleading advertisements to Grand Wireless customers in attempt to lure them away from the plaintiff's stores.[8] The court reasoned that an arbitration clause would be a meaningless arrangement if its terms did not extend to employees, because businesses can operate only through their employees.

Nevertheless, this doctrine is far from a rubber stamp. In 2017 the same First Circuit court held that a delivery driver employee was not entitled to coverage under his employer's arbitration clause. In *Ouadani v. TF*, a delivery driver brought suit against Dynamex after they terminated his employment. Ouadani, whose compensation was paid by SBS in agreement with Dynamex, sought to avail himself of the companies' arbitration agreement. The court here held that, while the arbitration clause applies to agents, "Ouadani is not, in this context, bringing his wage-and-hour claims as an agent 'acting on behalf of SBS.'"[9] This comparison highlights the truly fact-dependent nature of the agency doctrine—and for that matter, all of these third-party contract doctrines.

Veil Piercing/Alter Ego

Veil piercing in arbitration is like any other veil piercing exercise. When a corporate relationship between a parent and its subsidiary is sufficiently close as to justify piercing the corporate veil and holding one corporation legally accountable for actions of another, that third-party parent can be brought under the arbitration clause of a subsidiary. However, as in litigation, a corporate relationship alone does

---

7. *See, e.g.*, Grand Wireless, Inc., v. Verizon Wireless, Inc., 748 F.3d (1st Cir. 2014).

8. *Id.*

9. *Ouadani*, 876 F.3d at 37.

not provide a basis for allowing enforcement against a nonsignatory. Courts operate under the presumption of separateness, and the burden falls to the party requesting to join a party to the arbitration to prove this is not the case. While every state has slightly different case law, a parent company must generally dominate and control the affairs of a subsidiary so that it is not independent to apply this method.

Take *Keystone Shipping v. Textport Oil,* for example. There, the Southern District of New York held that a subsidiary could be held to arbitrate under a parent's clause where parties had failed to respect the corporate veil,[10] but Keystone, which only alleged that it was affiliated with the party with whom Textport signed an arbitration agreement and nothing more, could not overcome this presumption of separateness.[11]

Third-Party Beneficiary and Estoppel

If you benefit from a contract, can you be forced to arbitrate under it? Again, this classic contract principle applies equally to litigation and arbitration. Third-party beneficiary law usually presents in arbitration in one of two circumstances: either the nonsignatory beneficiary can compel arbitration between signatories (third-party beneficiary), or the signatories can compel a third party to arbitrate (estoppel). In either instance, courts will look to whether the contract containing the arbitration clause reflects an intent to confer a direct benefit on another party. If this is true, and the third party has knowledge of this agreement, a court is very likely to require this third-party beneficiary to arbitrate.

In sum, a party looking to bring in a nonparty as a third-party beneficiary or estoppel must generally prove the following:

- The nonsignatory received direct and substantial benefits from the agreement containing the arbitration clause;
- The underlying agreement manifests an intent to confer specific legal rights upon the nonsignatory; and

10. Keystone Shipping Co. v. Textport Oil Co., 782 F. Supp. 28 (S.D.N.Y. 1992).
11. *Id.* at 32.

- In instances involving a third-party beneficiary, the party had knowledge of the agreement's existence.

The circumstances surrounding *Flexi Van Leasing v. Through Transp. Mut. Ins.* illustrate the kind of situation in which a court would find both of these elements satisfied in the case where a third-party beneficiary is attempting to avail itself of a contract to which it was not a party.[12] There, plaintiff Flexi Van required its Korean client to purchase insurance before they were able to lease vehicles from the plaintiff. The client purchased the requisite insurance—the contract for which happened to include an arbitration clause—and then promptly went bankrupt. Flexi Van made a claim for failed payments through the client's insurance and requested to arbitrate these claims under the contract. The insurance company resisted, reasoning that because their contract was with the client and not Flexi Van, Flexi Van could not avail themselves of a contract to which it was not a party. The Third Circuit disagreed. Flexi Van was held to have knowingly and purposefully derived benefits from its customer's insurance company; it was clearly the intended third-party beneficiary of the contract and could avail itself of the arbitration clause.

Estoppel cases are equally fact intensive. In *AD v. Credit One*, the daughter of a cardholder sued Credit One after the credit card company bombarded her with debt collection calls aimed at her mother in alleged violation of the Telephone Consumer Protection Act.[13] While the plaintiff did not have a contract with Credit One, the card company attempted to compel arbitration under the plaintiff's mother's agreement. The court found this was a no-go: the plaintiff did not derive enough of a benefit from her mother's card contract to compel her to arbitrate.

12. Flexi Van Leasing, Inc. v. Through Transp. Mut. Ins. Ass'n, 108 F. App'x 35 (3d. Cir. 2004).

13. A.D. v. Credit Once Bank, N.A., 885 F.3d 1054 (7th Cir. 2018).

CHAPTER 10

Injunctions

What happens when your client's contract has an arbitration clause but the situation is an emergency? Maybe a key employee with a noncompete has gone across the street with the client's customer lists to work for a competitor. Maybe the client's intellectual property is being pirated. Maybe a key supplier has stopped delivering. In any of these instances, the client is not going to want to hear about institutional rules, appointment of arbitrators, and the scheduling conference by which every step in the arbitration is laid out for the next nine to twelve months. Not a chance. That client is going to want to know one thing: how do we get relief NOW?

This confronts the alternative dispute mechanism of arbitration with a problem. By definition, an arbitral panel takes time to materialize; opposing parties must connect, review a panel list of arbitrators, choose from this list of arbitrators, agree on the chosen arbitrators, convene the panel—the list goes on. And, of course, a dispute does not simply pause during this period; trade secrets continue to leak, critical supply chains disintegrate, and a whole host of other emergencies ensue while the arbitral panel is being built.

If the parties run to court instead of arbitration, then the emergency situation is dealt with but the arbitration clause is ignored—in direct contravention of the arbitration presumption and pro-arbitration bias in our court system and as examined earlier in this book. But if the parties stay in arbitration, how do you deal with the emergency?

Over the last generation, a practical and widely accepted solution to this problem has emerged. Parties who claim an emergency can BEGIN in court. Upon establishment of the classic standards (especially irreparable injury and likelihood of success on the merits, etc.) for emergency equitable relief, the court can award such relief. This is particularly the case where the court is being asked to freeze the status quo rather than to issue an order commanding that one or more parties take action (a so-called permissive rather than mandatory injunction).

But that's it. That is the extent of the court's role. The ultimate determination of the merits of a dispute that parties previously committed to resolution by arbitration must still be determined by arbitration. The practice pointer here if you find yourself between the rock and the hard place of an arbitration clause and an emergency is to commence the arbitration, show the court (yes, court) that you are not making an end run around the arbitration clause, but then seek emergency relief in court and make clear that you are seeking only to preserve the status quo pending the arbitrator's merits decision. Much of the jurisprudence on this issue involves disputes as to whether the injunction remedy is "ultimate merits" or just "status quo." Set your papers up in advance to make it clear that you are only seeking interim relief necessary to preserve the status quo, so that the arbitrator can ultimately rule on the merits of the dispute. And, if you are on the flip side and want to block the injunction request and keep the dispute entirely in arbitration, focus on the relief sought and try to characterize your opponent as committing the entire case, all at once, to the court in violation of the arbitration clause.

The Hollow Formality Doctrine

The key to success in arbitration injunctions is to show a court that by the time an arbitrator gets around to the dispute, it will be too late and the irreparable injury would have occurred, to the destruction of your client's interests. Courts have found that equitable relief prior to arbitration is warranted when, if no action were to be taken while the panel was being constituted, subsequent arbitration or relief granted by the arbitrator would be worthless. As the Sixth Circuit put it in the oft-quoted *Performance Unlimited v. Questar Publishers* case:

> A grant of preliminary injunctive relief pending arbitration is particularly appropriate . . . where the withholding of injunctive relief would render the process of arbitration meaningless or a hollow formality, because an arbitral award, at the time it was rendered, could not return the parties substantially to the status quo ante.[1]

The *Performance Unlimited* court held that, even in a dispute subject to mandatory arbitration under the FAA, a district court has subject matter jurisdiction under section 3 of the FAA to grant preliminary injunctive relief "provided that the party seeking the relief satisfies the four criteria which are prerequisites to the grant of such relief."[2] As with litigation, arbitrating parties must prove (1) irreparable injury in the absence of an injunction, (2) that the threatened injury to the moving party outweighs any harm created by an injunction against the nonmoving party, (3) the injunction is not adverse to public interest, and (4) the moving party has a substantial likelihood of success on the merits in order to qualify for injunctive relief from the court. Common examples of where arbitration without preliminary equitable relief would constitute a "hollow formality" include these:

- A party will have gone out of business or fail to exist.
- The subject matter of the arbitration (business relationships, trade secrets, facilities, etc.) will be destroyed.

However, practitioners should note that whether or not an arbitration would be a hollow formality for the purposes of injunctive relief in no way relates to the merits of the case.

---

1. Performance Unlimited v. Questar Publishers, 52 F.3d 1373, 1380 (6th Cir. 1995).
2. *Id.*

The Injunction Carveout

Parties, particularly those who believe that there might come to be an emergency situation in their contractual relationship (for example, the licensing of sensitive intellectual property), can also engage in self-help in advance, through the drafting of the arbitration clause. This is especially prudent because, while the Hollow Formality Doctrine is the majority rule among circuit courts (the First, Second, Third, Fourth, Fifth, Sixth, Seventh, and Ninth Circuits all recognize that the FAA provides courts with jurisdiction to grant a preliminary injunction in order to preserve the status quo in matters that otherwise mandate arbitration), the rule is not universal.

That takes us to drafting. The best way to show a court that an emergency injunction request does not violate the parties' commitment to arbitration is to provide for an emergency court injunction remedy in the dispute resolution (arbitration) clause itself. That resolves any question of intent and avoids a battle of colliding doctrines, and it reduces the dispute to whether there is a genuine emergency. This is known as an injunction carveout.

What Is an Injunction Carveout?

An injunction carveout is a section of the arbitration clause that provides for outside injunctive relief in the event of an emergency situation. Where an arbitration agreement generally encompasses "all disputes related to or arising out of the present contract," this carveout ensures that a court or a pre-created injunction tribunal can address time sensitive issues while the arbitration is being constituted. Executed well, a clearly written injunction carveout leaves no question as to who has jurisdiction to handle these emergent circumstances.

Drafting the Injunction Carveout

When drafting a carveout, parties should keep a few points in mind. Any carveout should make clear that it is an *exception* to the arbitration clause. Terms such as "notwithstanding" or "except" easily check this box and make clear that bringing an injunction issue to court does not waive the parties' right to arbitrate. An injunction carveout does not need to be a drawn out or overcomplicated to be effective, either. Take, for example, the clause at issue in *Henry Schein, Inc. v. Archer*:

> Any dispute arising under or related to this agreement (except for actions seeking injunctive relief and disputes related to trademarks, trade secrets, or other intellectual property of [party]), shall be resolved by binding arbitration in accordance with the arbitration rules of the American Arbitration Association.[3]

This carveout is relatively effective, highlighting "actions seeking injunctive relief" as an exception to the general arbitration clause. Parties might also choose to enumerate the courts that have jurisdiction to grant such relief:

> Notwithstanding the arbitration clause, [a party] may bring an action for injunctive relief in any court having jurisdiction to enforce a party's non-competition, trademark, and/or proprietary rights, in order to avoid irreparable harm.[4]

A party can also choose to make the injunction carveout its own standalone paragraph:

> *Injunctive Relief:* Notwithstanding the foregoing, each party shall be permitted to institute proceedings in a federal or state court of competent jurisdiction to seek temporary or preliminary injunctive relief to maintain the status quo in any dispute arising out of or relating to this Agreement pending the resolution of that dispute through arbitration.[5]

However, be sure to avoid the pitfalls of an *overbroad* injunction carveout, which can have unintended effects as well. Parties should restrict their clauses to "injunctive relief" or "preliminary injunctions" rather than "equitable relief" as a whole. After all, "equitable relief" can come in many forms, and a nonspecific carveout can leave the

---

3. Henry Schein, Inc. v. Archer & White Sales, Inc., 139 S. Ct. 524 (2019).

4. Toddle Inn Franchising, LLC v, KPJ Assocs., LLC, 8 F.4th 56, 65 n.11 (1st Cir. 2021).

5. MATT ADLER, COMMERCIAL ARBITRATION: CASES, PROBLEMS AND PRACTICE (2d ed., Carolina Academic Press 2021).

unwary party fighting off attempts to litigate requests for specific performance or repayment.

If the Hollow Formality Doctrine Exists, Why Include an Injunction Carveout in the Arbitration Clause?

Lawyers often opt for a belt and suspenders. Such an approach is warranted in this case. Providing courts with express consent to intervene under prescribed circumstances is always a good idea in any jurisdiction. If the court does subscribe to the Hollow Formality Doctrine, an express stipulation makes clear to the court that the tribunal is not the exclusive remedy in these situations and precludes any discussion on the topic, thus saving litigation costs. On the flip side, if the court does not subscribe to this doctrine, a carveout clause is even more essential; arbitration is a creature of contract, and an arbitration clause will generally be enforced as written.

Institutional Rules and Arbitrator Injunctions

The potential conflict between arbitration and emergency relief can also be addressed when the parties choose institutional arbitration (as a reminder from earlier chapters, an example would be an arbitration clause that commits the dispute to AAA or JAMS). Most institutional rules confer upon arbitrators the jurisdiction to grant equitable measures, including the ability to award injunctive relief. However, this is little help to parties when the tribunal does not exist. To bridge this gap and provide parties an alternative to the public courts, many institutions provide for the appointment of an emergency arbitrator or panel.

The AAA, for example, will appoint a separate emergency arbitrator capable of ordering emergency equitable relief:

> Rule 38: Emergency Measures of Protection
>
> * * *
>
> (c) Within one business day of receipt of notice [. . .] the AAA shall appoint a single emergency arbitrator designated to rule on emergency applications. The

> emergency arbitrator shall immediately disclose any circumstance likely, on the basis of the facts disclosed on the application, to affect such arbitrator's impartiality or independence. Any challenge to the appointment of the emergency arbitrator must be made within one business day of the communication by the AAA to the parties of the appointment of the emergency arbitrator and the circumstances disclosed.

The ICC not only allows for a similar appointment of an emergency arbitrator but also includes a separate set of rules governing this arbitrator so they do not interfere with the jurisdiction of the tribunal in the process of creation provided for in the parties' contract:

> Article 29: Emergency Arbitrators
>
> (1) A party that needs urgent interim or conservatory measures that cannot await the constitution of an arbitral tribunal ("Emergency Measures") may make an application for such measures pursuant to the Emergency Arbitrator Rules in Appendix V. Any such application shall be accepted only if it is received by the Secretariat prior to the transmission of the file to the arbitral tribunal pursuant to Article 16 and irrespective of whether the party making the application has already submitted its Request for Arbitration.
>
> * * *
>
> (3) The emergency arbitrator's order shall not bind the arbitral tribunal with respect to any question, issue or dispute determined in the order. The arbitral tribunal may modify, terminate or annul the order or any modification thereto made by the emergency arbitrator.

JAMS, too, provides for the appointment of an emergency arbitrator to help parties in emergencies:

> Rule 2. Party Self-Determination and Emergency Relief Procedures
>
> * * *

(ii) JAMS shall promptly appoint an Emergency Arbitrator to rule on the emergency request. In most cases the appointment of an Emergency Arbitrator will be done within 24 hours of receipt of the request. The Emergency Arbitrator shall promptly disclose any circumstance likely, based on information disclosed in the application, to affect the Arbitrator's ability to be impartial or independent. Any challenge to the appointment of the Emergency Arbitrator shall be made within 24 hours of the disclosures by the Emergency Arbitrator. JAMS will promptly review and decide any such challenge. JAMS' decision shall be final.

Although institutions have taken steps to ensure parties can arbitrate their emergency injunction proceedings even before their contracted arbitral tribunal is constituted, does this mean parties *must* take these issues to the emergency arbitrators provided? The institutions themselves have answered with a resounding "no"—AAA Rule 37, ICC Article 28, and JAMS Rule 24 all note that their respective rules are not incompatible with the adjudication of interim measures in court, suggesting that subscribing to an institutional rule set does not mean that those parties must arbitrate injunctive relief requests. Courts, on the other hand, are more divided. The Ninth Circuit, for example, held in *Toyo Tire* that parties who have the option to use an emergency arbitrator may nonetheless choose to bring their injunction dispute to the courts.[6] But six years later, a Northern District of California court held the exact opposite: that parties must take advantage of emergency arbitrators available to them when seeking an injunction before petitioning the court.[7] This, unfortunately, is another area where practitioners simply need to be aware of the law in their presiding district.

So, when faced with a choice between institutional, arbitrator emergency relief and emergency relief by a court, which should you

6. Toyo Tire Holdings of Ams., Inc. v. Cont'l Tire N. Am., Inc., 609 F.3d 975 (9th Cir. 2010).

7. Smart Techs v. Rapt Touch Ir. Ltd., 197 F. Supp. 3d 1204 (N.D. Cal. 2016).

choose? Prudent parties usually choose the latter. This is because, by definition, the need for emergency injunctive relief generally arises in a situation where minutes and hours, not even days, matter greatly. Injunction papers can be prepared, served, and filed immediately, and an emergency judge is always on duty. Moreover, any special injunction issued by an arbitrator may be challengeable in court anyway. While the institutional availability of emergency injunction procedures is a positive development, at this time the safest course is to proceed immediately to court. If the court then orders you back to arbitration and indeed to institutional arbitration, so be it, but it usually makes sense to start in court.

CHAPTER 11

Consolidation and Waiver

We come now to two of the smaller procedural, yet nonetheless important, issues facing arbitrating parties. First, what of consolidations? Can two arbitrations be combined to provide for a more efficient dispute resolution? And second, even if parties have signed an arbitration contract, is it possible to waive the right to arbitrate altogether?

Consolidation

Multi-party disputes are not uncommon. Your client may be litigating against both a contractor and a subcontractor, or against both a supplier and a manufacturer. Litigation rules provide for devices such as joinder and even consolidation. In arbitration, this is more difficult. Arbitration clauses, as we have reviewed, are case by case, contract by contract, and party by party. It is not uncommon to have a business situation in which, even if there are arbitration clauses in all of the relevant contracts with all the relevant parties, those clauses may have been negotiated at different times, by parties with different bargaining power, and so can provide for arbitration in different places with different rules and choices of law. Your client may find itself having to arbitrate in Los Angeles against one party and in New York against another, yet it is the same ultimate dispute (and you will want everyone at the settlement table).

In such situations, consolidation of the arbitration would be the most efficient outcome. Arbitration rules, however, can be clumsy here, and there are threshold questions about who has the authority to order the consolidation. We review these below. As always, the advice remains to try to achieve consensus on these battles, absent which—as is often inevitable—you may be faced with a preliminary battle about where and how the main battle takes place.

When Does Consolidation Occur?

The question of arbitral consolidation can arise in one of three different scenarios:

- The same parties find themselves in multiple disputes arising from different contracts or transactions, each with its own arbitration clause (this occurs when two parties have multiple agreements under which they conduct business, such as a sales agreement and a manufacturing agreement);
- Different parties bringing disputes to arbitration arising out of the same transaction (this happens in the context of business contracts or class arbitration); and
- The same parties in a dispute regarding the same transaction, but each party sues the other.

Who Decides to Consolidate Arbitrations?

In each of these three scenarios, separate contracts provided for separate arbitrations. So who has the power to prevent duplicative proceedings? Just as with arbitrator selection, discovery, or the number of arbitrators, parties can provide rules for consolidation in their arbitration clause (though this is rare) or agree to consolidate their arbitration with another after the dispute arises. Essentially if the parties can agree at almost any stage to consolidate their cases, that consent governs. But what happens when, as is often the case, parties do not agree? Does the question go to the court or to the arbitrators?

The Supreme Court has held that the question of what *kind* of arbitration takes place is a procedural issue for the arbitrator to decide.[1] As a result, the First Circuit has said that consolidation of all arbitral matters is a question of procedure reserved for arbitrator determination, not the courts.[2] The Third Circuit followed suit in *Certain Underwriters at Lloyds, London v. Westchester Fire Ins. Co.*, proclaiming that the question of consolidation was a procedural one meant for dissolution through the arbitrators themselves:

> In light of the above authority, the parties' agreement to arbitrate their disputes, contractual silence as to the consolidation issue, and the longstanding federal policy favoring arbitration, we see no reason why this procedural issue should not be resolved in arbitration.[3]

The Seventh and Eight Circuits also treat consolidation as a question for the arbitrator, and while not all circuits have yet to formally address the issue, this is considered the majority rule.[4]

As a result, it can pay dividends for parties to include consolidation procedures (or elect an institutional regime that contains them already) in certain contracts. Consider the situation surrounding your agreement: Are you drafting one contract of a group (say, separate manufacturing, sales, and distribution contracts)? Is your contract the most recent in a series of renewals? Can you foresee separate disputes arising from multiple contracts in any capacity? If so, you may want to consider including consolidation rules. The institutional rules below give examples of how some parties elect to handle this issue.

---

1. Howsam v. Dean Witter Reynolds, 537 U.S. 79, 84, 123 S. Ct. 588, 592 (2002); *see also* Green Tree Fin. Corp. v. Bazzle, 539 U.S. 444, 452, 123 S. Ct. 2402, 156 L. Ed. 2d 414 (2003).
2. Shaw's Supermarkets, Inc. v. United Food & Commer. Workers Union, Lo-Cal 791, 321 F.3d 251, 254 (1st Cir. 2003).
3. Certain Underwriters at Lloyd's London v. Westchester Fire Ins. Co., 489 F.3d 580, 590 (3d Cir. 2007).
4. *See, e.g.*, Blue Cross Blue Shield of Massachusetts, Inc. v. BCS Ins. Co., 671 F.3d 635, 636 (7th Cir. 2011); Avon Products, Inc. v. International Union, United Auto Workers, 386 F.2d 651 (8th Cir. 1967).

Institutional Rules on Consolidation

Many institutional rules do not address consolidation, but those that do, do it in style. Each in its own way provides for the arbitrators, or the institutions themselves, to decide whether consolidation is warranted.

JAMS Rule 6 on Preliminary and Administrative Matters, for example, leaves the question to the institution, but only in the event of three enumerated circumstances:

* * *

> (e) Unless the Parties' Agreement or applicable law provides otherwise, JAMS, if it determines that the Arbitrations so filed have common issues of fact or law, may consolidate Arbitrations in the following instances:
>
> (i) If a Party files more than one Arbitration with JAMS, JAMS may consolidate two or more of the Arbitrations into a single Arbitration.
>
> (ii) Where a Demand or Demands for Arbitration is or are submitted naming Parties already involved in another Arbitration or Arbitrations pending under these Rules, JAMS may decide that the new case or cases shall be consolidated into one or more of the pending proceedings and referred to one of the Arbitrators or panels of Arbitrators already appointed.
>
> (iii) Where a Demand or Demands for Arbitration is or are submitted naming Parties that are not identical to the Parties in the existing Arbitration or Arbitrations, JAMS may decide that the new case or cases shall be consolidated into one or more of the pending proceedings and referred to one of the Arbitrators or panels of Arbitrators already appointed.
>
> When rendering its decision, JAMS will take into account all circumstances, including the links between the cases and the progress already made in the existing Arbitrations. Unless applicable law provides otherwise, where JAMS decides to consolidate a proceeding into a pending Arbitration, the Parties

to the consolidated case or cases will be deemed to have waived their right to designate an Arbitrator as well as any contractual provision with respect to the site of the Arbitration.

Oftentimes, these rules delegate the task of determining whether consolidation is warranted, and, if so, which arbitrators should proceed, to an outside party. After all, one or more arbitrators will be reduced if their panel is consolidated with another. Relegating the decision to a third party makes the process easier and prevents even the most repressed self-interest from clouding the deciding arbitrator's judgment. International Centre for Dispute Resolution (ICDR) article 9, for example, provides for the appointment of a special "consolidation arbitrator" to determine whether cases should be combined.

Article 9: Consolidation

1. At the request of a party or on its own initiative, the Administrator may appoint a consolidation arbitrator, who will have the power to consolidate two or more arbitrations pending under these Rules, or these and other arbitration rules administered by the AAA or ICDR, into a single arbitration where:
   a. the parties have expressly agreed to appoint a consolidation arbitrator; or
   b. all of the claims and counterclaims in the arbitrations are made under the same arbitration agreement; or
   c. the claims, counterclaims, or setoffs in the arbitrations are made under more than one arbitration agreement; the arbitrations involve the same or related parties; the disputes in the arbitrations arise in connection with the same legal relationship; and the arbitration agreements may be compatible.
2. A consolidation arbitrator shall be appointed as follows:
   a. The Administrator shall notify the parties in writing of its intention to appoint a consolidation arbitrator and invite the parties to agree upon a

procedure for the appointment of a consolidation arbitrator.

b. If the parties have not within 15 days of such notice agreed upon a procedure for appointment of a consolidation arbitrator, the Administrator shall appoint the consolidation arbitrator.

c. Absent the agreement of all parties, the consolidation arbitrator shall not be an arbitrator who is appointed to any pending arbitration subject to potential consolidation under this Article.

d. The provisions of Articles 14-16 of these Rules shall apply to the appointment of the consolidation arbitrator.

3. In deciding whether to consolidate, the consolidation arbitrator shall consult the parties, may consult the arbitral tribunal(s), and may take into account all relevant circumstances, including:

   a. applicable law;

   b. whether one or more arbitrators have been appointed in more than one of the arbitrations and, if so, whether the same or different persons have been appointed;

   c. the progress already made in the arbitrations;

   d. whether the arbitrations raise common issues of law and/or facts; and

   e. whether the consolidation of the arbitrations would serve the interests of justice and efficiency.

4. The consolidation arbitrator may order that any or all arbitrations subject to potential consolidation be stayed pending a ruling on a request for consolidation.

5. When arbitrations are consolidated, they shall be consolidated into the arbitration that commenced first, unless otherwise agreed by all parties or the consolidation arbitrator decides otherwise.

6. Where the consolidation arbitrator decides to consolidate an arbitration with one or more other

arbitrations, each party in those arbitrations shall be deemed to have waived its right to appoint an arbitrator. The consolidation arbitrator may revoke the appointment of any arbitrators and may select one of the previously-appointed tribunals to serve in the consolidated proceeding. The Administrator shall, as necessary, complete the appointment of the tribunal in the consolidated proceeding. Absent the agreement of all parties, the consolidation arbitrator shall not be appointed in the consolidated proceedings.

7. The decision as to consolidation, which need not include a statement of reasons, shall be rendered within 15 days of the date for final submissions on consolidation.

AAA Rule 8 provides a hybrid approach to deciding joinder: either appointing a separate consolidation arbitrator or allowing the first-appointed arbitrator of the two disputes to decide consolidation.

(a) Consolidation

i) Two or more arbitrations may be consolidated if all parties to all of the arbitrations to be consolidated so agree.

ii) Unless all parties agree to consolidation, the party requesting consolidation of two or more arbitrations must file with the AAA and serve on all other parties a written request for consolidation with the supporting reasons for such request within 90 days of the date the AAA determines that all administrative filing requirements were satisfied for the last-filed case that is part of the consolidation request. Such time limit may be extended by the arbitrator appointed in the first-filed case upon a showing of good cause for the late request. The other parties to the arbitrations shall provide their written responses to the consolidation request within 10 calendar days after the AAA sends notice of receipt of the request.

iii) At its discretion, the AAA either may direct that the consolidation request be decided by the arbitrator appointed in the first-filed case or may appoint a consolidation arbitrator for the sole purpose of deciding the consolidation request.

iv) The arbitrator deciding consolidation may order consolidation of two or more cases for all purposes or for such limited purposes and under such conditions as the arbitrator may direct.

v) Absent agreement of all parties, an arbitrator appointed for the sole purpose of deciding the consolidation request shall have no further power to act, and shall be removed from the case, after the consolidation request is decided.

vi) In deciding whether to consolidate, the arbitrator or consolidation arbitrator shall take into account all relevant circumstances, including:

a) the terms and compatibility of the agreements to arbitrate,

b) applicable law,

c) the timeliness of the request to consolidate and the progress already made in the arbitrations,

d) whether the arbitrations raise common issues of law and/or fact, and

e) whether consolidation of the arbitrations would serve the interests of justice and efficiency.

While consolidation is not a universal issue, savvy drafters should consider whether it is more likely to occur in their particular context, whether their elected institutional rules provide for it, and whether they should supplement these rules with their own procedures.

Waiver

We saw in the opening chapters of this book that there can be disputes about whether a particular case is subject to arbitration. But when should that challenge be brought? Or, put differently, can a party be accused of shopping around and first litigating certain issues but only then seeking arbitration? Is that too late?

Start with the principle that arbitration is at bottom a contractual issue—and so, as with any contract, the exercise of rights under an arbitration clause is subject to waiver of those rights. Straying too far and for too long down the litigation path can result in a waiver of the right to arbitrate. Put differently, once in litigation a party may have to *stay* in litigation.

Each circuit has its own threshold for what constitutes waiver. While the Sixth Circuit "will not lightly infer a party's waiver of its right to arbitration," that court has held it may find waiver where a party (1) takes actions completely inconsistent with any reliance on an arbitration agreement and (2) delays its assertion to such an extent that the opposing party incurs actual prejudice.[5] Take *Solo v. UPS*, for example. There, Solo sued UPS in court; UPS moved to dismiss the lawsuit on the merits.[6] Only when the appellate court reversed the grant of dismissal did UPS then move to compel arbitration. The Sixth Circuit held this was too little too late—at bottom,"[a] party cannot keep its right to demand arbitration in reserve indefinitely while it pursues a decision on the merits before the district court."[7]

The First Circuit applies a different set of factors when determining if a waiver occurred, namely:

> whether the party has actually participated in the lawsuit or has taken other action inconsistent with his right, . . . whether the litigation machinery has been substantially invoked and the parties were well into preparation of a lawsuit by the time an intention to arbitrate was communicated by the defendant to the plaintiff, . . . whether there has been a long delay in seeking the stay or whether the enforcement of arbitration was brought up when trial was near at hand. . . .

5. Hurley v. Deutsche Bank Tr. Co. Ams., 610 F.3d 334, 338 (6th Cir. 2010).

6. Solo v. UPS Co., 947 F.3d 968, 976 (6th Cir. 2020)

7. *Id.* (citing MC Asset Recovery LLC v. Castex Energy, Inc. (*In re* Mirant Corp.), 613 F.3d 584, 591 (5th Cir. 2010)).

> Other relevant factors are whether the defendants have invoked the jurisdiction of the court by filing a counterclaim without asking for a stay of the proceedings, . . . whether important intervening steps (e.g., taking advantage of judicial discovery procedures not available in arbitration . . .) had taken place, . . . and whether the other party was affected, misled, or prejudiced by the delay. . . .[8]

As a result, when ruling in cases with similar fact patterns to those in *Solo*, the First Circuit has found no waiver on the part of the compelling party. In *Creative Solutions Group v. Pentzer Corp.*, for example, the defendant moved to compel arbitration two months after it was required to plead to the complaint and five months after plaintiffs filed the action. The First Circuit found no waiver, holding "it could hardly be said that 'the litigation machinery had been substantially invoked and the parties were well into preparation of a lawsuit' by the time an intention to arbitrate was communicated."[9]

There may, however, be "hybrid" situations where a party has to take certain actions in court but these are so preliminary so as to not constitute litigation of the merits of the dispute. An example might be an action to preserve documents or to demand production of documents under a statutory right.[10] In neither case is the court being asked to do anything other than as a preliminary step. Arguments of waiver should not succeed here.

Parties should take care to check the waiver law and precedent in their jurisdiction before settling on legal strategy where they may want to invoke arbitration.

8. Creative Sols. Grp. v. Pentzer Corp., 252 F.3d 28, 32 (1st Cir. 2001).

9. *Id.* at 33.

10. *See, e.g.*, Lobster 207, LLC v. Pettegrow, No. 1:19-CV-00552-LEW, 2020 U.S. Dist. LEXIS 95561 (D. Me. June 1, 2020) (finding defendant did not waive his right to compel arbitration where defendant filed a waiver of service, requested production of documents to enable a response to a motion for attachment, and waited four months before moving to compel arbitration, because defendant was affected by service issues and COVID delays, and plaintiff had not "worked the oars" long enough to be prejudiced by compelling arbitration).

CHAPTER 12

Enforcement

You've done all the work. You've drafted the arbitration clause, compelled arbitration, arbitrated, and won. The arbitrator hands you their reasoned award (which you made sure to stipulate to in your well-written clause), awarding your requested relief. Now what?

Enforcement is perhaps the most important aspect of arbitration. As you saw with third-party subpoenas, arbitrators' power extends only as far as the parties who provided their consent. Arbitrators have the ability to order certain relief, but they possess no real-world way to compel enforcement. As a result, parties must confirm their awards with the court. A confirmed arbitration award contains the same weight and enforceability as any other federal judgment. FAA sections 9, 10, 11, and 12 govern the enforcement of arbitration awards. This chapter will examine each in turn.

Enforcing an Award

FAA section 9, which governs initial enforcement of awards, provides as follows:

> If the parties in their agreement have agreed that a judgment of the court shall be entered upon the award made pursuant to the arbitration, and shall specify the court, then at any time within one year after the award is made any party to the arbitration may apply to the court so specified for an order confirming the award, and thereupon the court must grant such

an order unless the award is vacated, modified, or corrected as prescribed in sections 10 and 11 of this title. If no court is specified in the agreement of the parties, then such application may be made to the United States court in and for the district within which such award was made. Notice of the application shall be served upon the adverse party, and thereupon the court shall have jurisdiction of such party as though he had appeared generally in the proceeding. If the adverse party is a resident of the district within which the award was made, such service shall be made upon the adverse party or his attorney as prescribed by law for service of notice of motion in an action in the same court. If the adverse party shall be a nonresident, then the notice of the application shall be served by the marshal of any district within which the adverse party may be found in like manner as other process of the court.

The important takeaways from section 9 are threefold.

1. **Include a confirmation plan in your arbitration clause.** Section 9 deliberately allows parties to preemptively enumerate the courts with the ability to confirm their arbitration award. Parties can specify one particular court to which a confirmation application must be made or extend this ability to any court of competent jurisdiction. The ability to choose your confirming court can come in handy when your arbitration is seated somewhere other than where the respondent's assets are located, or simply when logistical issues make it easier to confirm an award somewhere other than the seat. Providing which court has the right to enforce the award may be even more important if the arbitration takes place outside the United States. If the parties' clause does not enumerate the court(s) in which an arbitration award can be confirmed, an award can be confirmed *only* in the district court for the district in which the award was made.
2. **An arbitral award must be confirmed within a year of issuance.** Do not let this window expire. A court is not required to confirm (and, save for extenuating circumstances, will not

confirm) an arbitration award after a year. Best practice is to file a petition to enforce an arbitral award with the court as soon as possible after an arbitrator provides a ruling.

3. **Arbitral awards are almost always enforced.** Section 9 requires a court to grant an order confirming an arbitration award unless the award is vacated, modified, or corrected. As explained below, vacation of an arbitral award is very rare.

The Mechanics of Enforcement

If the losing party does not contest the arbitrator's ruling, the winning party should file a section 9 petition to confirm. The district court will enter the order, and the confirmed award can be enforced as any other federal judgment.[1]

Challenging an Award

Arbitral awards are incredibly difficult to challenge. FAA section 10, which governs the circumstances in which parties can challenge arbitration awards, provides an *exhaustive* list of only four grounds that will give rise to vacatur. Section 10 reads, in its entirety:

> (a) In any of the following cases the United States court in and for the district wherein the award was made may make an order vacating the award upon the application of any party to the arbitration—
> (1) where the award was procured by corruption, fraud, or undue means;
> (2) where there was evident partiality or corruption in the arbitrators, or either of them;
> (3) where the arbitrators were guilty of misconduct in refusing to postpone the hearing, upon sufficient cause shown, or in refusing to hear evidence pertinent and

1. For an example of these mechanics in action, *see* Bonar v. Dean Witter Reynolds, Inc., 835 F.3d 1378 (11th Cir. 1988).

material to the controversy; or of any other misbehavior by which the rights of any party have been prejudiced; or

(4) where the arbitrators exceeded their powers, or so imperfectly executed them that a mutual, final, and definite award upon the subject matter submitted was not made.

(b) If an award is vacated and the time within which the agreement required the award to be made has not expired, the court may, in its discretion, direct a rehearing by the arbitrators.

(c) The United States district court for the district wherein an award was made that was issued pursuant to section 580 of title 5 may make an order vacating the award upon the application of a person, other than a party to the arbitration, who is adversely affected or aggrieved by the award, if the use of arbitration or the award is clearly inconsistent with the factors set forth in section 572 of title 5.

First and foremost, note that section 10(a) does not mention an arbitrator's legal error as a reason for vacatur. This is because legal error on the part of the arbitrator is not sufficient grounds for a court to deny enforcement of an arbitration award. In short, "[t]he arbitrator's construction holds, however good, bad, or ugly."[2]

This is an integral difference between litigation and arbitration: while litigation allows for multiple tiers of appeal, arbitrating parties have few avenues available to challenge final rulings and *no recourse* in the event an arbitrator interprets the contract incorrectly or applies the wrong law altogether.[3] As the Second Circuit once put it,

> The role of a district court in reviewing an arbitration award is "narrowly limited" and "arbitration panel determinations are generally accorded great deference under the FAA" . . . .

2. Oxford Health Plans LLC v. Sutter, 569 U.S. 564, 573, 133 S. Ct. 2064, 2071 (2013).

3. *See, e.g.*, Brentwood Medical Associates v. UMWA, 396 F.3d 237 (3d Cir. 2005) (affirming an arbitration award even though it was explicitly predicated on language that was not in the contract).

Consequently, the burden of proof necessary to avoid confirmation of an arbitration award is very high, and a district court will enforce the award as long as "there is a barely colorable justification for the outcome reached."[4]

At bottom, unless the parties can prove one of the four enumerated circumstances in section 10(a) has occurred, the award will be confirmed. So what, exactly, will get an award thrown out?

Section 10(a)(1): "Procured by Fraud, Corruption, or Undue Means"

To vacate an arbitration award based on fraud, a movant must satisfy the widely accepted three-part test, proving:

1. The respondent engaged in fraudulent activity,
2. The fraud was not discoverable upon the exercise of due diligence prior to or during the arbitration, and
3. The fraud materially related to the outcome of the arbitration.[5]

While each circuit varies slightly in the phrasing of its test, the bar to prove fraud is high, and it must be "abundantly clear" that the award was a product of fraud, corruption, or undue means.[6] In *Floridians for Solar Choice v. PCI Consultants*, for example, the court found that a party's changing damages theory did not meet the strict definition of fraud under section 10(a)(1).[7] There, the movant argued that the court should vacate the award because the respondent had represented it sought less than $500,000 in damages during the hearing, but in its post-hearing briefing it argued that it sought damages for the entire

4. Kolel Beth Yechiel Mechil of Tartikov, Inc. v. YLL Irrevocable Tr., 729 F.3d 99, 103–04 (2d Cir. 2013) (citations omitted).

5. Bonar v. Dean Witter Reynolds, Inc., 835 F.2d 1378 (11th Cir. 1988). To prove corruption, some courts require parties to prove a "intentional misconduct" that "measures equal in gravity to bribery, corruption, or physical threat to an arbitrator." Liberty Sec. Corp. v. Fetcho, 114 F. Supp. 2d 1319, 1321 (S.D. Fla. 2000).

6. Envtl. Chem. Corp. v. Coastal Envtl. Grp., Inc., 2018 U.S. Dist. LEXIS 157246, at *18 (S.D.N.Y. Sep. 14, 2018).

7. Floridians for Solar Choice v. PCI Consultants, Inc., 314 F. Supp. 3d 1346, 1355 (S.D. Fla. 2018).

contract price. The court held that the movant had failed to show the opposing party defrauded or used undue means to influence the arbitrator, and that a change in damages theory did not amount to fraud.

Furthermore, because of general deference provided to the arbitrator's decision, courts will not recognize evident fraud as a reason for vacatur. As the *Floridians* court noted, "even if the Court considered [movant's] change in damages theory sufficient to demonstrate fraud or undue means, 'vacatur is precluded . . . where the arbitrators had before them all material information relating to the alleged undue means.'"[8] This is because an arbitrator would have had to be aware of evident fraud and proceeded to grant their award anyway. Generally, courts find vacatur proper only in extreme circumstances where an arbitrator was not privy to—but made a decision based on—fraud, such as when an expert testifies under false credentials.[9]

Section 10(a)(2): "Evident Partiality"

As arbitrators are oftentimes also practitioners, there is a fine line between arbitrators who are truly partial and arbitrators who are simply experienced and connected in their field. Each circuit provides its own test for determining evident partiality, but to vacate an award, all agree that movants must prove (1) more than the mere appearance of bias and (2) a direct connection between bias and the outcome of an arbitration.[10] An arbitrator's failure to disclose a connection with a party is another hallmark of evident partiality.[11] An undisclosed father-son relationship between an arbitrator and the party union president,

8. *Id. (citing* Liberty Sec. Corp. v. Fetcho, 114 F. Supp. 2d 1319, 1321 (S.D. Fla. 2000)).

9. *See, e.g.*, Bonar v. Dean Witter Reynolds, Inc., 835 F.2d 1378 (11th Cir. 1988).

10. *See, e.g.*, Certain Underwriting Members of Lloyds of London v. Florida, 892 F.3d 501, 2018 A.M.C. 1719, 2018 U.S. App. LEXIS 15377 (2d Cir. 2018); Health Services Management Corp. v. Hughes, 975 F.2d 1253, 23 Fed. R. Serv. 3d (Callaghan) 1175, 1992 U.S. App. LEXIS 22419 (7th Cir. 1992).

11. World Bus. Paradise, Inc., v. Suntrust Bank, 403 F. App'x 468, 470 (11th Cir. 2010); Tenaska Energy, Inc. v. Ponderosa Pine Energy, LLC, 437 S.W.3d 518, 524 (Tex. 2014).

for example, is certainly grounds for vacatur.[12] Substantial financial interest in the outcome of an arbitration is often another dead ringer for evident partiality; for example, the Supreme Court ordered the vacatur of an award rendered by a neutral third-party arbitrator where he failed to disclose one party was a large customer of his business.[13]

A Note on Timing

Timing matters when raising an evident partiality challenge. As discussed briefly in Chapter 5, a party who does not raise the issue of evident partiality at the time it is discovered runs the risk of waiving the ability to raise the issue at all. In *Ergobilt v. Neutral Posture Ergonomics*, a Northern District of Texas court refused to vacate an arbitral award for evident partiality where the arbitrator had disclosed a longstanding relationship with the defendant, but the opposing party did not register its opposition on the record when the issue was originally discovered.[14] While it is best practice for parties to register their objection to a partial arbitrator as soon as they discover an issue, the FAA does not provide for pre-award removal of an arbitrator.[15] It is important to confirm your circuit's position on removing biased arbitrators and balance the pros and cons of submitting the issue to the courts pre-award. Alternatively, parties may be better served raising the issue with the governing institution, if they have one, rather than a court.

Section 10(a)(3): "Failure to Allow Evidence"

Failure to allow evidence is one of the most common ways to seek vacatur of an arbitral award. In fact, so common are section 10(a)(3) challenges that arbitrators often preemptively admit more evidence than they would otherwise, in order to avoid their awards being

12. Morelite Constr. Corp. v. N.Y.C. Dist. Council Carpenters Ben. Funds, 748 F.2d 79 (2d Cir. 1984).
13. Commonwealth Coatings Corp. v. Cont'l Cas. Co., 393 U.S. 145 (1968).
14. ErgoBilt, Inc. v. Neutral Posture Ergonomics, Inc., Civil Action No. 3:97-CV-2548-L, 2002 U.S. Dist. LEXIS 12459, at *17 (N.D. Tex. July 9, 2002).
15. Savers Prop. & Cas. Ins. Co. v. Nat'l Union Fire Ins. Co., 748 F.3d 708, 720 (6th Cir. 2014).

subsequently vacated in court. Courts mount a purely procedural inquiry in weighing a section 10(a)(3) objection.

An arbitrator does not need to hear all the evidence tendered by the parties to withstand a section 10(a)(3) inquiry. Rather, they must only give an adequate opportunity for each party to present their case and allow a fair hearing.[16] In *White v. Valero Ref. New Orleans*, for example, the plaintiff moved to vacate an award after the arbitrator prohibited him from deposing individuals who assisted in the preparation of an investigation report and then allowed the report into evidence. The Fifth Circuit court denied the plaintiff's motion to vacate, noting that the inability to take a deposition did not deprive him of a fair hearing:

> The arbitrator is not bound to hear all of the evidence tendered by the parties; however, he must give each of the parties to the dispute an adequate opportunity to present its evidence and argument. An evidentiary error must be one that is not simply an error of law, but which so affects the rights of a party that it may be said that he was deprived of a fair hearing.[17]

Of course, different circuits interpret the rule differently. In *Hoteles Condado Beach, La Concha & Convention Ctr. v. Union de Tronquistas Local 901*, a First Circuit court found an arbitrator correctly admitted evidence in a case regarding an employee-employer dispute but failed to give that evidence enough weight in his decision-making process.[18] In disregarding essential evidence, the court held that arbitrator had violated section 10(a)(3) and vacated his award. In short, be sure to consult your local precedent to determine the requirements of successful section 10(a)(3) arguments in your district.

---

16. White v. Valero Ref. New Orleans, LLC, No. 11-1014, 2013 U.S. Dist. LEXIS 86158, at *2 (E.D. La. June 19, 2013).

17. *Id.*

18. Hoteles Condado Beach, La Concha & Convention Ctr. v. Union de Tronquistas Local 901, 763 F.2d 34, 36 (1st Cir. 1985).

Section 10(a)(4): "Exceeded Power"

Section 10(a)(4) is another often-pled reason for requesting vacatur. Despite its reputation as a catch-all category for parties looking to challenge an award that fails to meet the hallmarks required by section 10(a)(1–3), section 10(a)(4) also imposes a high bar. As SCOTUS articulated in *Stolt-Nielsen, S.A. v. Animal Feeds Int'l*, "[i]t is only when [an] arbitrator strays from interpretation and application of the agreement and effectively 'dispense[s] his own brand of industrial justice' that his decision may be unenforceable [under § 10(a)(4)]."[19] In determining whether an arbitrator has, in fact, dispensed their own brand of industrial justice, courts typically look to the parties' contract to determine whether it was disregarded altogether.[20]

It is worth noting that an arbitrator's deviation from the parties' contractual interpretation does *not* an unenforceable award make. In *Barclays Capital Inc. v. Platt*, for example, former Barclays investors attempted to vacate an arbitration award after the arbitrator forgave debt owned by respondents, arguing "there is no basis in the promissory notes, applicable rule or decision derived from the FAA, or any body of law that 'authorizes the Notes to be "forgiven."'"[21] The court ruled that this was not a question of the arbitrator's complete disregard of the contract, because the interpretation of the promissory notes was properly before the arbitral panel according to the arbitration clause. Rather, "[m]ovant's basis for vacatur, while made pursuant 9 U.S.C. § 10(a)(4), asks this Court to do exactly what it is not permitted to do—'look to the legal merits of the underlying award.'"[22]

While the reasoning of the arbitrator regarding these merits is generally beyond reproach, courts may find arbitrators exceeded their powers where they directly contradict the plain language of a contract

19. Stolt-Nielsen S.A. v. AnimalFeeds Int'l Corp., 559 U.S. 662, 671, 130 S. Ct. 1758, 1767 (2010).

20. *Barclays Capital Inc. v. Platt,* No. 15-21850-CIV-MARTINEZ-GOODMAN, 2018 U.S. Dist. LEXIS 216879, at *11 (S.D. Fla. Dec. 21, 2018); *see also* Stolt-Nielsen S.A. v. AnimalFeeds Int'l Corp., 559 U.S. 662, 671, 130 S. Ct. 1758, 176 L. Ed. 2d 605 (2010)).

21. Barclays Capital Inc. v. Platt, 2018 U.S. Dist. LEXIS 216879, at *13.

22. *Id.*

itself.[23] These courts reason that the arbitrator is "confined to the interpretation and application of the collective bargaining agreement . . . . [and] although he may construe ambiguous contract language, he is without authority to disregard or modify plain and unambiguous provisions."[24] If you think this distinction appears unclear, you're not alone. In *Hoteles Condado*, the court found that the arbitrator's decision "manifested an infidelity to the plain and unambiguous terms of the contract between the parties" where he improperly applied a disciplinary rule contained in the contract. One could be forgiven for wondering if, by interpreting the parties' contract, the court is simply considering the merits of a case—the very thing it promised not to do.

The "exceeded powers" argument varies in interpretation between courts. Again, as above, it is best practice for practitioners to evaluate their local applicable case law.

Manifest Disregard: The Fifth Ground for Vacatur?

What happens if an award does not fit into any of the enumerated grounds in section 10 but is still just outright wrong? SCOTUS attempted to weigh in on this very question in *Hall Street Assocs. v. Mattel*. There, SCOTUS proclaimed the exhaustive nature of section 10, noting that it had previously prohibited parties from expanding upon the enumerated bases for vacating arbitration awards.[25] However, in the same breath, the Court also pondered the possibility of a fifth ground for vacatur: an arbitrator's "manifest disregard of the law." Breathing new life into the term from a 1958 SCOTUS case, the Court mused:

> Maybe the term "manifest disregard" was meant to name a new ground for review, but maybe it merely referred to the § 10 grounds collectively, rather than adding to them [. . .] or, as some courts have thought, "manifest disregard" may have

23. Hoteles Condado Beach, La Concha & Convention Ctr. v. Union de Tronquistas Local 901, 763 F.2d 34, 41 (1st Cir. 1985).

24. *Id.*

25. Hall St. Assocs., L.L.C. v. Mattel, Inc., 552 U.S. 576, 578, 128 S. Ct. 1396, 1400 (2008).

been shorthand for § 10(a)(3) or § 10(a)(4), the paragraphs authorizing vacatur when the arbitrators were "guilty of misconduct" or "exceeded their powers."[26]

Containing perhaps the most infamous "maybe" in American judicial history, *Hall Street* immediately split the circuit courts. On one side, the Second, Fourth, Seventh, Ninth, and Tenth Circuits interpret the ruling to mean that a court may set aside an arbitration award if it was rendered "in 'manifest disregard of the law' to such an extent that '(1) the arbitrators knew of a governing legal principle yet refused to apply it or ignored it altogether and (2) the law ignored by the arbitrators . . . [was] well defined, explicit, and clearly applicable.'"[27] In these circuits, disappointed parties often tack on a manifest disregard challenge to their underlying section 10 argument, but generally, inevitably, still fail to prevent enforcement. This is because, as emphasized above, to succeed in showing manifest disregard, a party must prove the arbitrator knew the law and then prove that he or she actively chose to ignore it. This is a very high bar indeed. Furthermore, given varying interpretations of the term among the manifest disregard camp itself, the concept is also in desperate need of clarification. Until this happens, courts will simply be asked to determine how bad an award needs to be before it becomes unacceptable.

On the other side, the Fifth, Eighth, and Eleventh Circuits do not recognize manifest disregard as a separate avenue to vacatur.[28] The Third Circuit is still undecided.[29] Some individual states have also incorporated manifest disregard into their state arbitration regulations (for example, in Georgia, O.C.G.A. 9-9-13 (2010) (b)(5) expressly states "the arbitrator's manifest disregard of the law" is grounds for vacatur).

---

26. *Id.* at 1404.

27. Hardy v. Walsh Manning Sec., L.L.C., 341 F.3d 126, 129 (2d Cir. 2003); *see also* Dewan v. Walia, 544 Fed. App'x 240 (4th Cir. 2013); Comedy Club, Inc., v. Improv West Assocs., 553 F.3d 1277 (9th Cir. 2009); Adviser Dealer Servs., Inc. v. Icon Advisers, Inc., 557 Fed. Appx. 714, 717 (10th Cir. 2014).

28. *See, e.g.*, Citigroup Global Mkts v. Bacon, 562 F.3d 349 (5th Cir. 2009); Paisely Park Enters v. Boxill, 371 F. Supp 3d 578 (D. Minn. 2019); Campbell's Foliage, Inc. v. Fed. Crop Ins. Corp., 562 F. App'x 828, 831 (11th Cir. 2014).

29. *See, e.g.*, Prospect CCMC, LLC v. CNNA/Pa. Ass'n of Staff Nurses & Allied Prods., Civ. Action No. 18-174, 2019 Dist. LEXIS 12714 (E.D. Pa. Jan. 28, 2019).

While manifest disregard may seem an attractive avenue for parties to challenge an award in those circuits that recognize this method of vacatur, the fact is that a manifest disregard challenge almost always fails, regardless of the court's standard. Because manifest disregard of the law is such a difficult action to allege, let alone prove, attorneys looking to bring this challenge should know that it is unlikely to work and should advise their clients of the likely outcome.

Correcting Mistakes in an Award

What happens if the arbitrator makes an honest mistake in rendering an award? Even arbitrators misplace a comma once in a while. Is there recourse if they accidentally award $1,000 in attorney's fees when the intended award was $100,000? Thankfully, yes. FAA section 11 governs the modification of arbitral awards after their completion. It provides:

> In either of the following cases the United States court in and for the district wherein the award was made may make an order modifying or correcting the award upon the application of any party to the arbitration—
>
> (a) Where there was an evident material miscalculation of figures or an evident material mistake in the description of any person, thing, or property referred to in the award.
>
> (b) Where the arbitrators have awarded upon a matter not submitted to them, unless it is a matter not affecting the merits of the decision upon the matter submitted.
>
> (c) Where the award is imperfect in matter of form not affecting the merits of the controversy.
>
> The order may modify and correct the award, so as to effect the intent thereof and promote justice between the parties.

The drafters of the FAA acknowledged that arbitrators are human and mistakes happen. Not only does this apply to mistakes like a misplaced comma or incorrect calculation, but also it applies to mistakes that become evident only after new evidence comes to light post-arbitration. In these instances, courts have found that where the mistake could change the outcome of an arbitration, courts have the power to amend the award "to do equity and justice."[30] For example, in *Transnitro v. M/V Wave*, an enforcing court saw an arbitration panel had made an evident mistake by not subtracting interest already paid from the total award. The court ruled that even though these errors were not the fault of the arbitrators (because evidence of the interest had not been presented to them), the court could still amend the ruling in the interest of fairness. Any party who sees a similar mistake may file a section 11 petition to correct it.

Practice Tip

When faced with an error, parties should act promptly to correct it, or move for confirmation of the award as-is.

You may wonder: why ask the court to fix an overt mistake? Can a party not simply return to the arbitrators and ask them to issue an amended award? Not exactly.

An arbitration panel cannot outlast its mandate. Just as a panel must be seemingly convened out of thin air when a dispute triggering its jurisdiction arises, so too must it seemingly evaporate when it has achieved its purpose: settling this dispute. After a panel has rendered its final award, it becomes "functus officio," meaning it no longer has any legal power, or even existence. It can therefore not correct any errors after the award.

Of course, there are exceptions to this general (borderline poetic) rule. The Second, Third, Fifth, Sixth, Seventh, and Ninth Circuits recognize an exception to functus officio where an arbitration award is ambiguous, and arbitrators are called upon to clarify their award.[31]

---

30. Transnitro, Inc. v. M/V Wave, 943 F.2d 471, 472 (4th Cir. 1991).

31. *See, e.g.*, Gen. Re Life Corp. v. Lincoln Nat'l Life Ins. Co., 909 F.3d 544 (2d Cir. 2018).

Arbitrators are also allowed to fix recent mistakes "apparent on the face of [their] award."[32]

Confidentiality and Confirmation of Awards

Arbitral awards must be confirmed by a court, which, by its nature, does not lend itself to confidentiality. As a result, parties should take care to provide as little confidential information in their section 9 petition to confirm an arbitration award.

While arbitration is known for its confidentiality, in some circumstances, courts may override this presumption of confidentiality in the interest of judicial transparency. For example, where the parties bring a section 10(a) petition for vacatur to the court, the documents provided in pursuit of vacatur may become public. In *Century Indemnity v. AXA Belgium*, an S.D.N.Y. court denied the parties' motion to file pleadings under seal, noting that judicial documents necessarily bring with them the implication of public access:

> [a] confidentiality agreement . . . may be binding on the parties, but it is not binding upon the Court. And while parties to an arbitration are generally "permitted to keep their private undertakings from the prying eyes of others," the "circumstance changes when a party seeks to enforce in federal court the fruits of their private agreement to arbitrate, i.e. the arbitration award. [. . .] In circumstances an arbitration award is confirmed, the public in the usual case has a right to know what the Court has done."[33]

In *Contship Containerlines v. PPG*, an S.D.N.Y. court further eliminated any idea of implied confidentiality when it subpoenaed relevant documents from a prior arbitration that would have otherwise remained private. The court noted that the need to resolve the

---

32. *See, e.g.*, Mid Atl. Capital Corp. v. Bien, 956 F.3d 1182 (10th Cir. 2020).
33. Century Indem. Co. v. AXA Belgium, 2012 U.S. Dist. LEXIS 136472, at *43 (S.D.N.Y. Sep. 24, 2012).

matter fairly and inexpensively outweighed the parties' need for confidentiality.[34]

Despite this trend, there are still steps parties can take to ensure as much confidentiality as possible. When drafting, parties can add a clause enumerating which documents must be filed with the court to confirm an award. This can preclude the filing of the full reasoned award itself, instead requiring just the arbitrator's decision and relief. The less information that must be filed with the court for simple confirmation, the better.

34. Contship Containerlines, Ltd. v. PPG Indus., Inc., 2003 U.S. Dist. LEXIS 6857, at *6 (S.D.N.Y. Apr. 17, 2003).

TABLE OF CASES

G

H

J

K

L

V

W

Z

INDEX